**50 YEARS OF
COVERT OPERATIONS
IN THE US**

About the cover

COVER DESIGN: Carole Caron

COVER IMAGES, COUNTERCLOCKWISE FROM TOP LEFT:

1. President Franklin Roosevelt, October 1937, delivering "Quarantine the Aggressor" speech, a turning point in the US rulers' political preparations for what would become the imperialist bloodbath of World War II. GETTY IMAGES

2. Ten thousand unemployed, organized by Teamster union leadership, defy police attack, demand increase in federal benefits, Minneapolis, Minnesota, April 1934. MINNESOTA HISTORICAL SOCIETY

3. Secret FBI document during World War II, targeting leaders of independence movement in US colony Puerto Rico.

4. Strike by sanitation workers in Memphis, Tennessee, 1968, during final stage of struggle consolidating defeat of Jim Crow anti-Black discrimination.

50 years of COVERT OPERATIONS in the US

LARRY SEIGLE · FARRELL DOBBS · STEVE CLARK

PATHFINDER
New York   London   Montreal   Sydney

Edited by Steve Clark

Copyright © 2014 by Pathfinder Press
All rights reserved.

ISBN 978-1-60488-063-2
Library of Congress Control Number 2014931671
Manufactured in Canada

First Edition, 2014
Fifth printing, 2023

The article "50 Years of Covert Operations in the US" by Larry Seigle first appeared under the title "Washington's Fifty-Year Domestic Contra Operation" in issue no. 6 (1987) of the Marxist magazine *New International*.

Pathfinder
www.pathfinderpress.com
Email: pathfinder@pathfinderpress.com

CONTENTS

Introduction
Steve Clark   7

50 years of covert operations in the US
Larry Seigle   25
Origins of FBI assault on Socialist Workers Party   29
Target: Fight for Black rights   39
Target: Labor movement   51
Frame-up in Minneapolis   57
McCarthy-era witch hunt   71
FBI's covert operations   81
Forcing the government operations to light   87
Why the Socialist Workers Party?   93
Expansion of political rights   103

Imperialist war and the working class
Farrell Dobbs   109

Notes   115

Index   121

INTRODUCTION

In August 1987 a federal district judge in New York City issued an injunction ordering that all documents obtained by the government in ways that violate the US Constitution and Bill of Rights cannot be "used, released, or disclosed" by the FBI or other federal police agencies.

The injunction came in connection with Judge Thomas Griesa's decision a year earlier, in August 1986, on a suit filed by the Socialist Workers Party in 1973. The party's aim was to bring into the open decades of covert spying and disruption against the SWP by the federal political police, and to mobilize opposition to these violations of the constitutional rights not only of members and supporters of the party and Young Socialist Alliance, but of other organizations and individuals targeted by covert government operations as well.

Although the Justice Department immediately filed notice after Griesa's 1986 decision that it would appeal, less than two years later the government withdrew its motion.

The fifteen-year-long battle by the Socialist Workers Party, backed by thousands, resulting in that federal court ruling marked a victory for the working class. Moreover, that victory stands and has a direct effect to this day, more than four decades after the suit was filed.

The opening article in this book—"Fifty Years of Covert Operations in the US: Washington's Political Police and the American Working Class" by Larry Seigle—provides an account of that political battle by the SWP and its allies. It was an unprecedented political initiative. A communist organization was filing *a suit* against the capitalist government, as opposed to being forced to defend itself and its members against *a case* trumped up by cops and prosecutors. Communist workers—along with fellow unionists, farmers, and supporters of civil rights—were *plaintiffs*, and government agencies and officials *defendants*. Not the other way around.

The broadly supported political campaign organized and led by the Socialist Workers Party provided an additional weapon that unionists, Black rights fighters, and others among the exploited and oppressed could use to better defend their own constitutional rights. Above all, it helped keep open political space for working people to speak, organize, and act outside the electoral and judicial arenas—to fight on our own terrain, in the factories, on the picket lines, and in the streets.

A few veteran communists—who had firsthand experience over decades with government frame-ups and attacks on militant workers—initially balked at such an undertaking. Wasn't a lawsuit just asking for trouble? Why set something in motion that will result in government depositions of party leaders? Why end up in a bourgeois courtroom by your own doing?

Such wariness was even greater among some former Communist Party members and others in the CP milieu whose dead-end Stalinist factionalism toward the SWP had ebbed over time, but who still recoiled at carrying out political activity openly as communists, much less in front of federal attorneys and a judge. Among other things, why expose your party's history and political record to public scrutiny?

But the SWP's central leaders, from those in the oldest

to newer generations, were convinced that attitudes were changing among workers and farmers in the United States as a result of the political conquests of the Black rights movement, anti–Vietnam War mobilizations, and other social struggles. The capitalist rulers and their government were on the defensive politically as a result of what was becoming known about cop spying, harassment, and disruption of working people and youth engaged in these fights. All this was compounded for the rulers in 1973 by the widely publicized "Watergate" revelations of rampant wiretapping and burglary by the Richard Nixon administration against its domestic rivals in capitalist politics.

All in all, the communist leaders concluded, conditions were unusually good for such a political campaign. The Socialist Workers Party never lies to working people, in the US or anywhere else in the world. Its history and political record are an open book. It has nothing to hide. As these conclusions were confirmed in life over the next fifteen years, initial doubts and hesitations were transformed into respect and support for the SWP's political course in this fight.

After more than seven years of pretrial discovery, the lawsuit went to trial in April 1981. The proceedings stretched out over twelve weeks. The court's sweeping 1986 decision in favor of the SWP's suit found no evidence "that any FBI informant ever reported an instance of planned or actual espionage, violence, [or] terrorism" by the party or its members. For the first time ever, a federal court ruled:

- that the use of FBI or other police informers to infiltrate organizations and spy on individuals engaged in political activity, including communists and other working-class militants, is a violation of the guarantee of privacy and freedom of association in the Bill of Rights (during the trial, the government acknowledged that the FBI alone—not counting the CIA, military intelligence, and other agencies among the defendants—had collected or stolen *10 million pages* of files on the socialists);

• that burglaries by the cops to steal or copy papers or plant microphones violate Fourth Amendment protections against "unreasonable searches and seizures" (the FBI admitted at least two hundred four "black bag jobs" of party offices just between 1945 and 1966); and

• that surreptitious disruption of party activity and the lives of its members and supporters is against the law (numerous examples of such harassment are described in *FBI on Trial: The Victory in the Socialist Workers Party Suit against Government Spying* edited by Margaret Jayko, and *Cointelpro: The FBI's Secret War on Political Freedom* by Nelson Blackstock, both published by Pathfinder).

Following up on those decisions, Griesa one year later issued his injunction "with respect to documents that the Government obtained through clearly illegal activities." The federal judge barred such files from being "used, released, or disclosed by defendants . . . for any reason except in compliance with an order issued by this court, applied for on notice, or in lawful response to a request under the Freedom of Information Act."

∼

Fifty Years of Covert Operations in the US was first published in 1987 in the Marxist magazine *New International*, and then the following year in Spanish as a small book. As the article indicates, it was written before all the matters in the suit had been finally decided by Judge Griesa in 1987 and before the government threw in the towel on appealing in 1988.

In the wake of this outcome of the SWP's fifteen-year battle came two other milestones in the party's long record of defending the political rights of working people, including its own members.

On March 4, 1988, Mark Curtis, an SWP member and worker at the Swift packinghouse in Des Moines, Iowa, was arrested and brutally beaten by cops only hours after taking part in a meeting to defend seventeen co-workers rounded up by immigration cops in a factory raid and threatened with deportation. He was framed up on rape and burglary charges and went to trial in September 1988. A broad international defense campaign called on Iowa authorities to drop the charges and then—following his conviction and sentencing to twenty-five years—to free Curtis from prison. He was released on parole in June 1996.

A week before the Curtis trial opened, the Socialist Workers Party registered a victory in another defense campaign, one it had been fighting for eleven years with widespread support. On August 31 the US State Department dropped once and for all the government's effort to deport Héctor Marroquín, a Mexican-born member of the Young Socialist Alliance and SWP and plaintiff in the party's lawsuit, and granted him permanent residency.

∼

The 1986 federal court decision that the president of the United States "cannot have discretion to behave unconstitutionally" stands today in face of the unrelenting expansion of executive and police powers during four Republican and Democratic presidencies since the ruling came down: those of George H.W. Bush, William Clinton, George W. Bush, and Barack Obama.

The Obama White House—and the meritocratic professional, academic, and other bourgeois-minded individuals from whom the administration enlists its staff and organizes its support—is taking this tendency to new heights. "Wherever we have an opportunity and I have the executive authority to go ahead and get some things done, we're just gonna go ahead and do 'em," the president said in a CBS "60 Minutes" interview in December 2011.

The record bears him out—from the acceleration (and political rationalization) of expanded Internet and phone wiretapping in the US and abroad; to the more than 400 "unacknowledged" murderous drone attacks since early 2009 in Pakistan, Yemen, and Somalia; to a sharp increase of deportations of immigrants and "silent sweeps" of workers without papers in factories and other workplaces; to IRS targeting of tax records of "Tea Party" and other conservative groups; to stepped-up surveillance of e-mail and phone records of journalists and criminal prosecution of their sources under the Espionage Act of 1917. This tendency can also be seen from the current administration's harsher penalties against US and foreign companies accused of violating Washington's embargo of Cuba, and unilaterally stiffened sanctions against Iran; to its circumvention of congressional review of presidential appointments and federal budget matters; to steeply escalated expansion and use of federal regulations, bypassing the need to submit new legislation for discussion and vote; and more.

∼

The victory in this long political battle by the Socialist Workers Party has bolstered its ongoing efforts since the mid-1970s to ensure the maximum possible protection for financial contributors to SWP campaigns, including campaigns for public office.

In April 2013 the Federal Election Commission extended for four more years the party's exemption from requirements that candidates must file names of both their contributors and vendors from whom they buy printing or do other business. The FEC ruling cited the 1986 federal court decision as well as some seventy declarations from workers and others who have supported communist candidates and public activities of the SWP. These declarations documented firings, police spying and harassment, and rightwing threats and assaults on the party and its members and supporters since 2009, when the previous FEC exemption had been granted.

The "government hostility and public and private harassment against the SWP was pervasive," the FEC ruled, and "thus continues to provide support for the SWP's current request" to extend the disclosure exemption it has fought for and won six times since 1974. This was a victory not only for the SWP but for all working people and for constitutional rights. It was the first successful push-back in some time by a working-class organization in face of years of escalating political, social, and economic "regulation" by employers and their government.

Among liberals, the crusade for political "transparency" and financial "disclosure" is a sacred cause. But it papers over fundamental class realities and conflicts—above all that not only all economic and financial power, but all political and military power too, rests in the hands of the capitalist class. That's the source of the hypocrisy about "transparency" and of the damage government-imposed "disclosure" inflicts on the exploited majority.

The demand for an end to secret state diplomacy, business secrets, and covert domestic cop-operations has been and remains part of the program of the communist movement. Each step toward putting an end to the ability of the propertied rulers to legally operate in secrecy is an advance for working people in the US.

Imposed on working-class parties such as the SWP, the unions, Black rights groups, or farm protest organizations, however, "disclosure" and "transparency" are instruments to unleash the capitalist government, cops, and right-wing outfits and individuals to probe, disrupt, and try to destroy the workers movement. They are a political obstacle to organizing effective defense of those threatened by government assaults and to mass independent working-class action to advance the interests of working people.

∼

Fifty Years of Covert Operations in the US points to the century-and-a-half-long proletarian course that made possible what the Socialist Workers Party accomplished through its political campaign to expose government spying and harassment and mobilize opposition to it. From the moment the SWP filed its lawsuit in 1973 through the 1981 trial and post-trial proceedings, the article says, the government

> kept trying to prove that the party said one thing in public and something different in its closed meetings. They tried to establish that the party maintained dual structures, one for public purposes and the other hidden from view. In every case, the facts showed the opposite. While a workers' party has the right, in fact the responsibility, to protect the privacy of its members and supporters from the bosses and the police, it has no right to keep its ideas, methods, and organizational concepts hidden from working people. . . .
>
> As the trial demonstrated, the FBI's accusations of conspiracy and hidden goals were *pure projection*. It turned out to be the White House and FBI, not the SWP, that conceal their aims and methods. It turned out to be the White House and FBI, not the SWP, that maintain a co-

vert structure to carry out what they cannot openly proclaim. It turned out to be the White House and FBI, not the SWP, that rely on conspiratorial modes of operation to achieve their goals behind the backs of the people of the United States.

The article traces the expansion of Washington's political police since US imperialism's repressive response, in the aftermath of World War I, to the Bolshevik-led October 1917 revolution in Russia and forging of the Communist International two years later—and their impact on workers and farmers in the United States who sought to emulate those revolutionary examples. The government's aim above all was to crush the newborn communist organizations in the US founded in 1919. (Already in those years, J. Edgar Hoover headed the Justice Department cop agency that targeted communist and anarchist workers, their organizations, and Black leaders such as Marcus Garvey and A. Philip Randolph. That agency became the Federal Bureau of Investigation in 1935, and Hoover remained its director until his death in 1972.)

This book puts a special focus on the Democratic administration of President Franklin Roosevelt in the late 1930s, as the US rulers prepared to enter the imperialist slaughter of World War II. It describes the growth and consolidation of the "national security" state in the wake of Washington's military, political, and economic victory in that war over its imperialist rivals, both "foes" (Germany, Austria, Italy, and Japan) and "allies" (the United Kingdom, France, and others).

The 1941 conviction and imprisonment of eighteen leaders of the Socialist Workers Party and class-struggle Teamsters leadership in Local 544-CIO in Minneapolis was a turning point in the buildup of US capital's political police. The frame-up was the Roosevelt administration's first use of the Smith "Gag" Act outlawing advocacy of revolutionary ideas, which the Democratic president had signed into law the previous year. The real "crime" of these working-class leaders was that they were effectively organizing political opposition within the unions to Roosevelt's drive to whip up popular support for the US rulers' war aims that workers and farmers would be sent to fight and die for.

During the 1981 trial of the SWP's lawsuit, a chief government witness, Robert Keuch, an associate deputy attorney general, was questioned by an attorney for the SWP about Roosevelt's 1939 executive order directing the FBI to step up its "investigation" of "subversive activities." Keuch replied that "there are simply ways that individuals and groups can act that may not necessarily constitute violations of the criminal statutes" (translation: that are legal even under US bourgeois law). The White House was concerned first and foremost about those "who were trying to influence public opinion to keep the United States out of war, to keep us neutral," the Justice Department official testified.

The "crime" of "trying to influence public opinion" about the coming war was sufficient for Roosevelt to shred the Bill of Rights.

This new edition includes the article "Imperialist War and the Working Class" by Farrell Dobbs, which deals with these origins of Washington's "covert war" at home. Dobbs was a convicted Smith Act defendant, a leader of the Teamster organizing drives in Minneapolis and the upper Midwest, and then a central leader of the SWP for decades. He wrote this piece in 1949 as an introduction to the third edition of *Socialism on Trial*, the trial testimony by SWP national secretary James P. Cannon.

Dobbs also recounts and condemns the Smith Act prosecution in New York in early 1949 of eleven leaders of the Communist Party, which is described in the opening article in this book. All were convicted, and ten were given the maximum sentence of five years. Dobbs, who covered this nine-month frame-up trial week in and week out for the *Militant* newspaper, points to the political blow the Communist Party leadership dealt to the working-class movement by its refusal to defend the first Smith Act defendants during the 1941 trial in Minnesota.

In fact, the CP leadership publicly welcomed the Minneapolis indictments and campaigned in the unions to quash support to the defendants. Earl Browder, the party's general secretary, and other CP leaders went so far as to prepare a dossier for the Justice Department in hopes of bolstering the government's case against the SWP leaders and union militants. Philip Jaffe, a former Communist Party leader, in the 1975 book *The Rise and Fall of American Communism*, details the contents of the dossier he received a copy of from Browder.

The CP leadership's trampling on elementary working-class solidarity is also recounted in the 1993 book *Advocate and Activist: Memoirs of an American Communist Lawyer* by John Abt, the party's longtime chief counsel and one of its leading cadres going back to the 1930s. The CP "made a terrible mistake in not defending the SWP" during the Minneapolis trial, Abt said.

Abt had accepted the CP leadership's course at the time, he acknowledged. "Little did we know," he said, "that in the postwar period the Smith Act would become the primary legal weapon to attack our Party and imprison its leaders."

Little did we know! The truth is that the SWP and Teamster defendants and their supporters explained this time and again to anyone who would listen in the labor movement (and many did, as shown by the endorsement of their defense effort, the Civil Rights Defense Committee, by some 150 international and local unions, representing over five million workers, as well as by hundreds of other individuals and organizations).

Some four decades later, Abt said, he participated in a meeting of the Communist Party's national leadership, urging it to support the SWP's lawsuit against federal police spying and harassment. He pointed to lessons from what the CP leadership had done in 1941. But Abt was voted down, "and the Party again refused to defend the SWP against government persecution."

∼

Another political conquest of the SWP's political campaign against the White House and federal police agencies is that Griesa's rulings made no distinction between party members and supporters who are US citizens and those who aren't. Both are covered by the decision and injunction (although the court took no position on concrete residency or deportation matters).

Among the federal agencies who were defendants in the party's suit was the US rulers' immigration police. At the time it was called the Immigration and Naturalization Service (INS). Today it's known as the Immigration and Customs Enforcement (ICE). Changing names notwithstanding, it is known and despised as *la migra* by working people who are its targets and by millions of others who know how the capitalists use it to divide and weaken the solidarity and fighting power of the working class, unions, and protests against discrimination of all kinds.

Deportations, in fact, were among the first and most brutal clubs wielded by bosses and their government in the repressive drive against the workers movement in the aftermath of World War I. In what became notorious as the Palmer Raids, named after the US attorney general at the time, more than 3,000 anarchists, communists, and other working-class militants were arrested and 750 deported in 1919 and 1920.

Since then repeated attempts by the rulers to use this weapon against cadres and leaders of the Socialist Workers Party have been fought back by the party, often mobilizing broad international support in the unions and among other supporters of political rights. In addition to the Héctor Marroquín case noted earlier, these have included unsuccessful attempts to deport:

• Carl Skoglund in the 1940s and 1950s, a Swedish-born founding leader of the communist movement and SWP and one of the eighteen imprisoned socialists and Teamster leaders during World War II;

• party member Joe Johnson, whose fight in the mid-1960s was waged using the pamphlet, *They Have Declared Me a Man without a Country*; and most recently

• Róger Calero, a Nicaraguan-born SWP leader and staff writer for the socialist newsweekly the *Militant* who in 2003 pushed back *la migra*'s efforts to deport him upon his return from a reporting trip to Cuba and Mexico and who won restoration of the permanent residence status he had had since 1989.

∼

For communist workers, defending ourselves is not primarily a question of legal arguments and courtroom tactics, although revolutionary-minded workers approach these matters with the utmost proletarian discipline and attention to detail.

Like everything else in the class struggle, how working people defend ourselves in face of frame-ups and other government assaults is above all a *political* question. It is part of the working class advancing along the revolutionary course toward replacing the state power of a tiny minority of propertied families—the dictatorship of capital—with that of the great majority, workers and farmers.

This has been true from the beginning of the modern working-class movement. Two outstanding examples can be singled out: the defense campaign led by Karl Marx and Frederick Engels well over one hundred sixty years ago to free eleven of their comrades framed up in Germany for "conspiracy" to overthrow the Prussian government after the defeat of the 1848–49 revolutions across Europe (what was known as the Cologne Communist Trial); and the amnesty campaign that in 1955 won the release of Fidel Castro and other combatants tried and convicted by the US-backed dictatorship in Cuba for their insurrectionary attack on the Santiago de Cuba and Bayamo army garrisons on July 26, 1953. The Moncada assault and the political course led by Castro, its principal organizer, opened the revolutionary struggle that would lead in 1959 to the triumph of the Cuban Revolution against the tyranny of Fulgencio Batista.

The trial testimony, courtroom statements, and other defense documents prepared by working-class leaders in the course of such battles are themselves often transformed into powerful instruments of revolutionary propaganda.

Such was the case with Karl Marx's *Revelations Concerning the Communist Trial in Cologne* written during and just after the 1852 trial in which seven of the eleven defendants were convicted. Marx proved the point in those pages that a "conspiracy" trial by the ruling class and its government "does not require any indictable action" and is "merely a pretext for burning political heretics in a legal way."

Such was the case with James P. Cannon's testimony at the 1941 Smith Act trial, published as *Socialism on Trial* and sold ever since as an introduction to the communist program.

Such was the case with Fidel Castro's prison reconstruction of his 1953 courtroom speech, *History Will Absolve Me*, which became the unofficial program of the July 26 Movement, clandestinely circulated in the thousands throughout Cuba during the revolutionary struggle.

Such was the case with Nelson Mandela's "I Am Prepared to Die," his statement from the dock at the 1964 trial that condemned him to prison for life as punishment for his leadership of the revolutionary fight to bring down South Africa's white supremacist regime.

As "Fifty Years of Covert Operations in the US" is being released in this new edition, working people in the United States and worldwide are learning about and being won in growing numbers to another international defense battle—the fight to free five Cuban revolutionists held behind bars in the US since 1998.

Gerardo Hernández, Ramón Labañino, Antonio Guerrero, Fernando González, and René González—known to millions as the Cuban Five—were railroaded to prison by Washington on a grab bag of trumped-up "conspiracy" charges. They had been gathering information for the Cuban government on plans by murderous Cuban American paramilitary groups in Florida that have operated with impunity on US soil, in order to help put a stop to violent attacks in Cuba, the United States, Puerto Rico, and elsewhere.

During their 2000–2001 trial and sentencing in Miami, the Five conducted themselves with pride and dignity as they defended their revolutionary principles and rebutted the charges fabricated against them by federal authorities. Above all, they refused to cop pleas. Each said at their sentencing hearings, and have repeated many times since, that he would act in the same way again in order to halt further deaths from assassinations and bombings. As Gerardo Hernández—given the most draconian of the sentences, a double life term—expressed it, "It is for this blood that I made the pledge to sacrifice even my own life."

Over the years since their incarceration, the Five have won the respect of fellow prisoners for their integrity, their daily leadership example, their consideration for others behind bars whose conditions they share as brothers, and their patient explanation of the Cuban Revolution whose proletarian internationalist and socialist values they exemplify in their political convictions and their conduct.

Neither the "capitalist justice" meted out to the Cuban Five over three administrations—Clinton, Bush, and Obama—nor the exemplary way the five revolutionaries have acted in face of it, are something new for the communist workers movement in the US and around the world. Jack Barnes, national secretary of the Socialist Workers Party, pointed to these realities of capitalist rule and the class struggle in a talk to a September 1988 rally in Des Moines, Iowa, on the eve of the opening of the trial of Mark Curtis.

"Mark Curtis will not get a fair trial," Barnes told the more than 400 participants in that meeting. "The courtroom is not where innocence and guilt will be decided, and it is not where justice will be found."

"The presumption of innocence has taken hundreds of years for working people to win," Barnes said. It is "one of the most important milestones on the march to human solidarity."

When workers are in the dock, however, from the point of view of the capitalist rulers, "It's the presumption of guilt that dominates in the 'democratic' United States," he said. The employers and their government "want workers in the meatpacking industry, paper workers, miners, workers of all kinds who will fight, to get the message that there are limits on your fighting."

That's why the worldwide defense campaign was so important, Barnes said. The capitalist rulers misjudge revolutionary-minded fighters, just as they misjudge the power of solidarity in the working class and among other defenders of political rights. Whatever the verdict at the trial, he insisted, "There is no way on earth they will succeed in their goal. They will not put Mark Curtis in prison for twenty-five years. They will not get him down on his knees.

"They will not prevent him from continuing to be the same person he is today, fighting for the same things, believing the same deeply held convictions, saying them openly to the entire world. He will continue to do all this, no matter where he finds himself, for however long."

That has been true for many thousands of working-class fighters who've been framed up and railroaded to prison along the long and winding revolutionary road toward power by workers and farmers in the US and the world over. It will remain true. And it's the most important lesson running throughout the pages of this book.

Steve Clark
January 2014

50 years of covert operations in the US

Larry Seigle

In late 1972, as the Watergate scandal was bringing to light previously hidden facts about the FBI's covert domestic operations, the leadership of the Socialist Workers Party made a proposal to Leonard Boudin, the country's foremost constitutional attorney and general counsel for the National Emergency Civil Liberties Committee.

The party suggested collaboration in a lawsuit against the FBI and other federal police agencies that would seek to establish that the SWP and the Young Socialist Alliance are entitled to engage in political activity without being spied on and infiltrated by agents provocateurs, having their phones tapped and their offices broken into, and being blacklisted and victimized in countless other ways by the political police.

The case would be at the center of a fight to establish that FBI operations against the SWP violate the First Amendment to the US Constitution, which guarantees freedom of speech and association, and the Fourth Amendment, which protects the privacy of individuals and organizations against arbitrary searches by government agents.

Such a case had never been brought before, Boudin was quick to point out. Defendants in criminal cases had often won acquittals based on government violations of their constitutional rights in arresting or prosecuting them. But there was precious little precedent for taking the offensive to counter FBI spying and disruption. In particular, no court had ever restricted the FBI's use of informers.

Nonetheless, Boudin agreed that the time was ripe for such an attempt. If sufficient public support could be mobilized, and the funds raised to finance such a massive undertaking, there was reason to believe that important gains for democratic rights could be won. And he stressed that rights won for the SWP and YSA—two communist groups—would strengthen the rights of everyone in this country and open a broader space for politics by working people seeking to defend themselves and advance their interests. This made the undertaking doubly worthwhile.

Boudin immediately began working to put the case together. The SWP started contacting other defenders of civil liberties to join in establishing the Political Rights Defense Fund, which would organize public support and raise funds for the battle in court. In July 1973 the case was filed in federal district court in Manhattan and assigned to Judge Thomas Griesa, a Republican appointed to the bench by President Richard Nixon.

Thirteen years later, in August 1986, Griesa handed down his opinion. The decision affirms the right of the Socialist Workers Party and Young Socialist Alliance to publicize their views and engage in political activity free from government interference. Griesa ruled—the first such ruling by a federal judge—that the FBI's use of undercover informers against the SWP violated the constitutional rights of the party and its members and supporters to privacy, an essential part of freedom of association. He also ruled that the FBI's covert break-ins of SWP offices and its disruption operations ("Cointelpros") were unconstitutional.

On that basis, Griesa ruled that the SWP is entitled to collect damages for the violations of these constitutional rights, totaling $264,000. And he ruled that the SWP will be granted an injunction making it illegal for federal agencies to make use of files containing information that was obtained by the FBI through means that the judge has ruled to be illegal.

Following the issuance of the injunction, Griesa will consider a motion by the SWP to require the Justice Department to pay several million dollars in attorneys' fees for the time put in by Boudin and the other lawyers who have worked on the suit. The issue of the attorneys' fees will itself be an important one: lawyers who vigorously defend the rights of communists have in the past often wound up themselves doing time for contempt of court or victimized in other ways. Collecting fees from the government for the work done on the SWP suit will be another substantial victory for democratic rights.

Lawyers for the Justice Department, headed by Attorney General Edwin Meese, are preparing the ground for their appeal of Griesa's decision, which seems certain to wind up in the United States Supreme Court. Supporters of the Political Rights Defense Fund are now undertaking a new round of activity to publicize the victory and its meaning and to rally support for the fight to defend the decision in the higher courts.

It is, therefore, an appropriate time to step back and look at the interconnections between this case and the broader fight by the unions and the Black movement in the United States to defend the right to organize and to expand the room for political activities free from government interference.

We will look at the origins and continuity of the FBI's covert war against the Socialist Workers Party. We will also attempt to answer some questions that this case has raised in the minds of many of its supporters. Why has the United States government organized such a massive assault on a small communist vanguard organization? Why has it been the Socialist Workers Party that took the lead in this initiative and has worked with others to carry it successfully to this point? Why not the Social Democrats, who have substantially greater resources and a larger following than the SWP? Why not the Communist Party, which has suffered more than the SWP from the FBI's illegal campaigns of spying, harassment, and disruption?

In tackling these questions, we will come up against some important problems of strategic perspectives for the working-class vanguard in the United States and for the broader international communist movement.

Origins of FBI assault on Socialist Workers Party

In the predawn hours of a Saturday in September 1939, FBI agents in Iowa and Nebraska simultaneously descended on the homes of union leaders in Omaha, Des Moines, and Sioux City. Teamsters union officials in the three cities were rousted from bed and placed under arrest. They were held on newly filed charges that accused them of burning a bakery truck during a strike in Sioux City more than a year earlier.

Acting under the direction of the US attorney general, the Justice Department in Washington, D.C., coordinated the FBI raids. The arrests occurred at a turning point in the US class struggle—a turning point whose significance became fully clear only much later.

The arrest of the Teamster leaders by the federal police marked the opening of the government's systematic use of the FBI as a weapon against class-conscious workers and farmers and against determined fighters against racist discrimination and national oppression in the United States.

The response to the raids and arrests also marked the opening of the fight by the working-class vanguard to mobilize all defenders of democratic rights to oppose the FBI's subversion of the Bill of Rights. That fight would soon deepen.

In 1941 the FBI and Department of Justice—in the first use of the newly adopted thought-control legislation, the Smith Act—would move directly against the Teamster organization in Minneapolis, a stronghold of Teamster union power and union democracy in the Midwest. The Minneapolis Teamster leaders were effective advocates of political independence of workers and farmers from the capitalist parties.

What was the background to the September 1939 arrests? A year earlier, bakery truck drivers in Sioux City, Iowa, organized in Teamsters Local 383, had struck the city's bakeries. They demanded higher wages and improvements in working conditions. The bosses charged that during the strike one of their trucks driven by a scab had been stopped and burned on a highway near the Iowa-Minnesota state line. The union denied any involvement. If in fact a truck had been damaged, the union pointed out, the employers probably did it themselves to undermine growing public support for the strike. The alleged incident was a brief sensation in local newspapers but was soon forgotten. Or so it seemed.

The bakery strike was won. The victory had a positive impact on the union movement throughout the Midwest. It came at a time when the Teamster-led effort to organize over-the-road drivers throughout the upper Mississippi Valley was making important strides. Several months after the strike victory, the International Brotherhood of Teamsters signed a one-year contract with the majority of freight operators in eleven Midwest states, covering more than 200,000 drivers and helpers.

The Teamster local officers charged with burning the

bakery truck were leaders of the strongest locals in this organizing drive. Only Local 383 in Sioux City had been involved in the bakery strike. But Local 90 in Des Moines, Iowa, and Local 554 in Omaha, Nebraska, were also decisive links in the multistate formation through which the over-the-road drive was being organized. That's why their leaders were included in the FBI's charges.

The nature of the frame-up became clear as soon as the trial opened in federal court in Sioux City. The case hinged on a procedural question: did the federal government have jurisdiction to try the union leaders, or were only state laws involved?

Justice Department lawyers offered testimony from FBI agents based on elaborate road surveys. The driver had been heading south from Minnesota to Iowa on a highway that made a ninety degree turn to the left near the state border, continued east for a few miles, and then made another right-angle turn south into Iowa. According to the FBI, by strange coincidence the truck just happened to have been halted at a place where the state line ran precisely down the middle of the road. The perpetrators stopped the truck on the Minnesota side of the road, the FBI witnesses testified, but then made the fatal mistake of moving the truck a few feet across the highway. As a result, it seems, they had transported a stolen vehicle across state lines—a federal crime. Accepting this ploy, the judge upheld the indictments.

"Their argument was as crooked as the road," wrote Farrell Dobbs in *Teamster Politics*, which tells the story of this frame-up trial and its importance in the developing antilabor offensive.[1*]

Nonetheless, an obliging judge and a biased jury bought the FBI testimony and Justice Department arguments.

* ENDNOTES BEGIN ON PAGE 115.

The seven defendants were convicted. Earl Carpenter, Jack Maloney, Francis Quinn, and Walter K. Stulz were sent to federal prison at Sandstone, Minnesota. Howard Fouts and Ralph Johnson were imprisoned in Terre Haute, Indiana. Louis Miller was assigned to Leavenworth, Kansas. All were given two-year terms.

The Teamsters organized a defense effort. In an appeal circulated to the labor movement and its supporters, Thomas Smith, secretary treasurer of Local 554 in Omaha, urged unionists and defenders of democratic rights to draw the lessons:

> In the interests of the union movement of the United States, we submit the record of FBI operations against the drivers' movement in the Middle West, with the hope that trade unionists everywhere will give these facts serious thought; and with the further hope that even now the weight of public opinion will cause the FBI to withdraw from its present road, a road which is surely leading to the development on American soil of the same sort of anti-labor political police which is the instrument of the ferocious dictatorships in Europe and Asia.

Smith's account of the facts and his appeal for support were published in the *Northwest Organizer,* voice of the Minneapolis Teamsters' local. The paper stressed that the Sioux City trial, together with other recent federal frame-ups of union activists, made it clear "that the FBI is systematically persecuting the labor movement as part of the Roosevelt government's preparations for dragging America into the war. Roosevelt wants first to crush the labor movement, especially its most successful and progressive sections."

Thomas Smith's warnings in the *Northwest Organizer* were right on the mark. The Sioux City frame-up signaled an important new development. For several years after the First World War, the FBI had functioned as a political police force, carrying out the arrest or deportation of some 3,000 unionists and political activists in 1919 and 1920 (the infamous "Palmer Raids"). But following widespread protests over these and other FBI actions, and with the decline of the postwar labor radicalization, the capitalist rulers decided against a federal secret police agency. They relied instead on city and state cops with well-established "bomb squads" and "radical units" and on state national guard units in cases of extreme necessity. These local and state agencies had intimate connections with antilabor "citizens" organizations organized by the employers and with hated private detective agencies, such as the Pinkertons, with long experience in union busting.

By the mid-1930s, however, a vast social movement was on the rise, with the Congress of Industrial Organizations (CIO) at the forefront. The relationship of forces was shifting in favor of working-class organizations. The bosses' old methods could no longer always be counted on. Communist perspectives did not come close to commanding majority support among working people, and in fact remained the views of a small minority, but the bosses were nonetheless concerned that progressive anticapitalist and anti-imperialist political positions advanced by class-struggle-minded union leaders were winning a hearing among a substantial section of the ranks of labor. Especially in times of crisis, such as war, minority points of view defended by established and respected working-class fighters could rapidly gain support.

With this in mind, the administration of President

Franklin Roosevelt expanded and centralized federal police power.

During and after the Watergate scandals of the mid-1970s, the immense scope of FBI disruption, spying, and provocations against the people of the United States came to light in an unprecedented way. But the origins of these operations are not—as most commentators place them—in the spread of McCarthyism in the 1950s or in Washington's attempts to disrupt the anti–Vietnam War movement and social protests of the 1960s.

The fact is that these FBI operations began on the eve of the Second World War. They were central to preparations by the US capitalist rulers to lead the nation into another carnage to promote their interests against their imperialist rivals and against the peoples of Asia, Africa, and Latin America struggling for liberation from colonial domination. These operations were directed against the leadership—and potential leadership—of the two major social forces in the United States that threatened to interfere with the ability of the US ruling families to accomplish their objectives: the labor unions and the Black movement. The government's aim was to isolate class-struggle leaders who could provide guidance to a broader movement that might develop.

World War II had begun in Europe in September 1939—just a few weeks before the arrests of the Teamster leaders in Iowa and Nebraska. On September 1 Germany's armed forces invaded Poland. Two days later the British and French governments declared war on Germany. Washington proclaimed neutrality and would maintain this as its stated policy until Japanese naval air forces attacked Pearl Harbor in December 1941. But official neutrality was a cover allowing the Roosevelt administration and Congress to take concrete steps toward entry into the war, while avoiding the nationwide public discussion that would have been set off by a Senate debate over a proposed declaration of war.

The drive toward war necessitated an assault on working people at home and against democratic rights in general. Roosevelt gave FBI chief J. Edgar Hoover free rein to use the FBI against the labor movement and Black organizations. The White House and Justice Department secretly authorized many of the illegal methods used by the FBI and turned a blind eye toward others.

This authorization for the FBI to assume the functions of a political police force was done without legislation, which would have had to be proposed and debated in Congress. It was accomplished instead by "executive order," a device that was rapidly assuming a major place in the operations of the government and would increasingly become a major mode of governing in the decades to come.

On September 6, 1939, Roosevelt issued an executive order directing the FBI "to take charge of investigative work" in matters relating to "espionage, counterespionage, sabotage, subversive activities and violations of the neutrality laws." The key phrase was "subversive activities," and the most important decision was to include this slippery concept in the list of responsibilities given the FBI. While there were federal laws against espionage, sabotage, and violation of US "neutrality," no law explained what "subversive activity" might consist of.

Two days later Roosevelt—again by executive decree—made a "finding" of the existence of a "national emergency." This allowed an increase in military spending without having to ask Congress for additional appropriations, thereby avoiding a sharpening public debate over the US government's march toward war. Simultaneously, the president ordered an expansion of the FBI's forces. His objective, Roosevelt told a news conference, was to avoid a repetition of "some of the things that happened" during World War I:

> There was sabotage; there was a great deal of propaganda by both belligerents, and a good many definite plans laid in this country by foreign governments to try to sway American public opinion.... It is to guard against that, and against the spread by any foreign nation of propaganda in this country which would tend to be subversive—I believe that is the word—of our form of government.

Forty years later, in a Foley Square courtroom in New York City, top Justice Department officials would cite Roosevelt's words as providing legal authority—derived from the president's "inherent powers" under the US Constitution—for the FBI's campaign of spying, disruption, and provocation against the Black movement, unions, and antiwar and women's liberation fighters and against communist organizations such as the Socialist Workers Party and Young Socialist Alliance.

As the trial of the SWP lawsuit unfolded during the spring of 1981 in Judge Griesa's courtroom, it became increasingly clear that the case revolved around issues far deeper than particular FBI abuses. The historical evolution of the FBI is part of a broader phenomenon in the United States. Underlying the threat today to the rights of privacy and freedom of association is the arbitrary rule by an expanding federal executive power. This power carries out policies at home and abroad that it is less and less able to openly proclaim or mobilize majority support for. It relies increasingly on covert methods to accomplish hidden or half-hidden objectives.

Among the government's chief witnesses at the trial in the SWP case was Robert Keuch, deputy assistant attorney general. At the time, Keuch was the third-ranking official in the Justice Department—one of those in the government who remain in place while other, more public, officials come and go with changes in administrations or other political shifts. When he spoke it was not with the voice of a particular administration but on behalf of a part of the state power itself.

Keuch's task on the witness stand was to make the case that the FBI's operations against the party, which span the decades since the SWP's founding convention in 1938, were constitutional because they had been authorized by the president. According to Keuch, the president of the United States has the "inherent power" under the Constitution "to protect our government against those who would seek to change it by unlawful means." This executive power is the source of the legal authority for "intelligence investigations" such as the one against the SWP. The purpose of such "investigations," Keuch testified, is to enable government officials "to take steps to protect ourselves[!] and protect our form of government. . . ."

According to Keuch, in 1939 President Roosevelt authorized the FBI to go after the SWP and other "subversives" because Roosevelt "wanted to know what were the activities and the aims and intentions of groups who potentially could be acting inimically to our form of government. . . ." When asked to define what "acting inimically" meant and how it differed from committing crimes, Keuch replied:

> Well, of course there can be many actions taken to attempt to influence the policies of the United States, its actions, et cetera, that do not necessarily involve or constitute a violation of law. It could be an attempt, for example, to

do away with the classification program [for secret government documents]. There could be agitation to do away with security programs totally. An intent to weaken the defenses of the United States. . . .

There are simply ways that individuals and groups can act that may not necessarily constitute violations of the criminal statutes. (Emphasis added.)

In other words, advocating ideas and taking actions that are not illegal—even as defined by reactionary legislation—but are nonetheless considered inimical to the interests of those in power can make you the target of the political police.

When asked what Roosevelt had in mind when he used the term "subversive," Keuch responded that the president had been referring first and foremost to those "who were trying to influence public opinion to keep the United States out of war, to keep us neutral." Roosevelt was targeting those who were exercising their constitutional right of free speech to oppose government policies.

There is a term for this concept of the authority to use police power to suppress political dissent and debate within the population: *totalitarianism*. It is exactly what Thomas Smith, the Omaha Teamster official, was warning against in 1939 when he sounded the alarm about the need to combat the emergence in the United States of "the same sort of anti-labor political police" used by repressive regimes in other countries.

Shining a spotlight on this genuinely totalitarian expansion of arbitrary rule by executive power, and laying bare its deep roots, has been one of the major accomplishments of the SWP case.

Target: Fight for Black rights

The employing class and its government set a high priority on isolating those who opposed the use of US military forces to defend capitalist interests overseas. The US rulers foresaw a war in which their vast empire would emerge dominant over its imperialist rivals, and after which they would rule unchallenged over peoples of color in the expanded parts of the globe staked out for US capital. Undisputed power in the "American Century" that they anticipated was beginning would allow them to rule without difficulty at home: holding the working class down and keeping "the colored" under control. At the same time, they hoped that the war launched by imperialist Germany against the Soviet Union would sufficiently weaken the workers' state to make possible its future overthrow and once again open that vast territory to capitalism.

As Washington prepared to enter the war under the banner of fighting the white-supremacist Nazi regime and its allies, Blacks in the United States were battling racist oppression. This struggle centered on the fight to overturn segregation, which existed not just in the South but in every federal government institution throughout the land and to a large extent in private industry and many aspects of social life.

During the decade of the Great Depression, Black working people had suffered even more than their white counterparts. Unemployment among workers who were Black was much higher than among workers who were white. Black farmers lost their land at an even higher rate than did white farmers. Education, health care, and other social services were qualitatively worse for Blacks.

In many parts of the country, particularly in the South, Blacks were systematically denied the right to vote. Segregation laws were backed up with extralegal terror to intimidate those who tried to organize to change these conditions. Lynchings were frequent in the Jim Crow South. The membership of racist terror outfits such as the Ku Klux Klan was intertwined with the cops, courts, and government officials. Throughout the country, police violence and frame-ups of Black defendants were widespread. Even the labor movement was segregated in much of the country. Many craft unions in the American Federation of Labor (AFL) organized to exclude Blacks from membership, and many AFL unions maintained separate locals for Blacks and whites in southern states.

The rise of the industrial union movement in the mid-1930s marked a big step forward in the struggle against segregation. The new industrial unions opened more doors for Black workers, often actively soliciting their participation in the unionization of basic industry. Militant Black workers had an opportunity to demonstrate their leadership capacities in many labor battles. But race barriers still existed, including within the labor movement itself.

On the eve of the war, the percentage of Black workers in basic industry was still quite low. Most plants engaged in war-related production still refused to hire workers who were Black. Federally funded job-training programs would not enroll Blacks on the grounds that war plants would not hire them anyway.

The US armed forces were segregated from top to bottom. Blacks were assigned to all-Black units under white officers or were relegated to be cooks, porters, laborers, or servants for the white officer corps. The idea of large numbers of Black soldiers in combat, let alone Black officers with the right to command on an equal basis with their white counterparts, was still unthinkable to the military brass and their superiors in Washington.

A measure of the degree of racism that Blacks faced in the military, and in society as a whole, was an order issued at an army camp in Pennsylvania at the beginning of the war. The camp commander proclaimed that "any association between the colored soldiers and white women, whether voluntary or not, would be considered rape." Under pressure from the NAACP, the War Department was forced in January 1942 to cancel the order.

More and more Black people decided that the time had come to step up the fight against this kind of racist oppression. If the United States had entered the war in the name of democracy and against Nazi doctrines of white race superiority, then the fight for changes at home could no longer be postponed. Moreover, as the war unfolded overseas, the rise of national liberation struggles, particularly in Asia and the Pacific, inspired confidence and greater militancy in the fight against racial oppression at home. While the imperialist powers fought each other over redivision of the planet, many colonial peoples seized the opportunity to advance the fight to take control of their own destinies.

Inside the United States, peoples of color likewise saw an opportunity to step up the fight for their rights.

The US rulers, however, portrayed the fight for equal rights for Blacks as "disruption of the war effort." Supporters of the government in the labor movement and in Black organizations argued that the battle against racism at home, while a worthy one, should nonetheless be kept in check until after a US victory in the war. The fight against racist discrimination, they argued, must not be allowed to go so far as to interfere with the "national unity" needed to win the war. This position was advanced by liberals, by the social democratic Socialist Party, and by the Stalinized Communist Party.

A growing number of Blacks, especially the youth, refused to accept this excuse for inaction. A young worker at an aircraft plant in Wichita, Kansas, captured the sentiment of this growing militancy in a letter published in January 1942 by one of the major newspapers aimed at Black people, the *Pittsburgh Courier*:

> Most of our leaders are suggesting that we sacrifice every other ambition to the paramount one, victory. With this I agree; but I also wonder if another victory could not be achieved at the same time. . . .
>
> Being an American of dark complexion . . . these questions flash through my mind: "Should I sacrifice my life to live half American?" "Will things be better for the next generation in the peace to follow?" "Would it be demanding too much to demand full citizenship rights in exchange for the sacrificing of my life?" "Is the kind of America I know worth defending?" . . .
>
> I suggest that while we keep defense and victory in the forefront that we don't lose sight of our fight for true democracy at home.

The V for victory sign is being displayed prominently in all so-called democratic countries which are fighting for victory over aggression, slavery and tyranny. If this V sign means that to those now engaged in this great conflict, then let we colored Americans adopt the double VV for a double victory. The first V for victory over our enemies from without, the second V for victory over our enemies from within. For surely those who perpetuate these ugly prejudices here are seeking to destroy our democratic form of government just as surely as the Axis forces.

The *Pittsburgh Courier* picked up this suggestion and launched what it called the "Double V" campaign. This campaign reverberated throughout the country, drawing its power from its expression of the determination among many Blacks not to accept continued postponement of their demands for full citizenship rights.

The FBI was working overtime to counter this growing civil rights fight. The facts about the FBI's crusade against the Black movement in this period unfortunately remain largely unknown and only sketchily documented publicly. What is known, however, makes it abundantly clear that the FBI's campaign of slander, frame-up, blackmail, and assassination against Malcolm X, Martin Luther King, the Black Panther Party, and other fighters for Black rights in the 1960s was not an aberration. It was the continuation of a course that began the day that the Roosevelt administration called on the FBI to go after "subversives."

In fact, from the standpoint of the Justice Department and FBI, the Black population as a whole was, if not subversive, at least suspect. The FBI prepared a secret wartime "Survey of Racial Conditions in the United States" for the benefit of the Roosevelt administration. In this 714-page report, the FBI explored the question—deeply troubling to them—of "why particular Negroes or groups of Negroes or Negro organizations have evidenced sentiments for other 'dark races' (mainly Japanese), or by what forces they were influenced to adopt in certain instances un-American ideologies."

The FBI survey concluded that while it might be going too far to say that "Negroes as a whole or the Negro people in a particular area are subversive or are influenced by anti-American forces . . . it must be pointed out that a number of Negroes and Negro groups have been the subjects of concentrated investigation made on the basis that they have repeatedly acted or have exhibited sentiments in a manner inimical to the Nation's war effort."

The FBI focused particular attention on newspapers such as the *Pittsburgh Courier*, whose nationwide circulation had skyrocketed with its Double V campaign. The report decried the fact that "the Negro press is a strong provocator of discontent among Negroes." (Like all cops, the FBI insists that "discontent" is created not by injustice and oppression but by instigators and agitators.) The secret FBI report went on to complain that the "general tone" of the Black press "is not at all, in many instances, informative or helpful to its own race. . . . More space is devoted to alleged instances of discrimination or mistreatment of Negroes than there is to matters which are educational or helpful."

To drive this point home to editors and writers for Black newspapers who insisted on saying things that were not "helpful," FBI agents began systematically visiting them. FBI agents also began calling on members of groups such as the NAACP, who were often enthusiastic supporters of the Double V campaign. The NAACP in particular, which was growing rapidly in size and activity, was targeted for infiltration by FBI stool pigeons and provocateurs. When fifteen Black sailors assigned as waiters for white officers in Washington, D.C., protested racial discrimination, the navy's response was to ask the FBI to investigate the protesters. The FBI obliged by opening a full-fledged, nationwide "investigation," including the massive use of informers, against the NAACP.

"FBI investigation of the NAACP [during the war] . . . produced massive information in Bureau files about the organization, its members, their legitimate activities to oppose racial discrimination, and internal disputes within some of the chapters," a US Senate committee concluded in 1975. But these "reports and their summaries contained little if any information about specific activities or planned activities in violation of federal law."

In mid-1942 Attorney General Francis Biddle summoned several editors of Black weeklies to Justice Department headquarters in Washington, D.C. Biddle arrogantly told the editors that their coverage of clashes between white and Black soldiers at army bases was a disservice to the war effort. Biddle did not challenge the accuracy of the reports but nonetheless insisted that the information should not have been printed. The attorney general, a liberal and staunch Roosevelt supporter, told the editors that if they did not change the tone of their papers, he was "going to shut them all up" on charges of sedition.

Then, according to one account of the meeting, Biddle picked up a copy of the *Chicago Defender* and

> complained about an article on nine black soldiers being transported through Alabama and having to wait twenty-two hours to eat because white restaurants in railroad stations would not feed them. Biddle said it would have been better if such an article had not appeared. In addition, he said, a number of the paper's other articles "came very

close to sedition," and the Justice Department was watching it closely "for seditious matter."[2]

Biddle's threats of prosecution for sedition did not come out of the blue. The editors he was threatening knew that leaders of the Teamster union and the Socialist Workers Party had been convicted in Minneapolis in 1941 for violation of the Smith Act, which outlawed advocacy of revolutionary ideas. In addition, sedition indictments had been brought in September 1942 against sixty-three members of the Temple of Islam (the Black Muslims), including its leader Elijah Muhammad. The Muslims were accused of sedition because they refused to accept the racist, anti-Japanese stereotypes that were a major part of US war propaganda and expressed solidarity with the Japanese as a people of color. Although the Justice Department could not make the sedition charge stick, it did succeed in convicting Elijah Muhammad and the other defendants on draft-evasion charges.

The government blocked shipment to troops overseas of Black newspapers that continued to publish condemnations of racism and other "unhelpful" facts and opinions. These papers were also often confiscated on military bases in the United States.

Early in 1943, at Biddle's urging, the US Post Office began proceedings to suspend the second-class mailing rights of several newspapers with uncompromising stands against race discrimination. These included the *Militant*, whose contributors and editors included members of the Socialist Workers Party. The Postmaster General banned the *Militant* from the mails on the grounds, among others, that its articles included "stimulation of race issues." All fighters for Black rights were supposed to get the point. The *Militant* won restoration of its mailing rights after a year-long battle that included the mobilization of protests from leaders of Black groups, trade unions, and civil liberties organizations.[3]

The race discrimination that Blacks fought against during the war had its counterpart in the treatment of other peoples of color at the hands of the government. While Mexican-American soldiers were not segregated into separate units, they nonetheless faced racist discrimination and abuse inside the US armed forces. In 1943 hundreds of Chicanos in Los Angeles were beaten up by cops and white vigilantes during several consecutive nights of a rampage through Mexican-American neighborhoods. Many of the racist gangs were made up of off-duty navy sailors or marines, but US military officials did nothing to stop the nightly attacks or punish those involved. Although none of the vigilantes were arrested, some seventy of their Chicano victims were picked up by the cops.

Exploitation of immigrant workers intensified during the war. In 1942 Washington began the so-called Bracero Program, which provided capitalist growers with a steady flow of superexploited immigrant farm labor from Mexico. The US government underwrote $120 million in costs to organize the teams that went to Mexico to recruit laborers and transport them into the United States during harvest seasons. These workers had no rights, were legally barred from joining unions, and were subject to deportation at their employers' whim.

The Bracero Program was in part designed to offset the upward pressure on agricultural wages caused by the internment of many Japanese American farm laborers in the months just after US entry into the war. These workers were among the more than 100,000 Japanese Americans interned during World War II.

This infamous action was carried out under the authority of an executive order issued by Roosevelt in February 1942. Roosevelt authorized military commanders to designate "military" areas "from which any or all persons may be excluded. . . ." This power was immediately used to declare California, Oregon, and Washington "strategic" areas. Every Japanese American living in those states was ordered into concentration camps. Compelled to settle their affairs in a matter of only days or a couple of weeks, they were forced to sell their farms, businesses, and homes at far below their market value. They were locked up in camps unfit for human habitation—not on the basis of anything they had done but on the grounds of their Japanese ancestry. Not only interned, they were thus expropriated to the benefit of the propertied classes.

In the US colony of Puerto Rico, many working people were unwilling to postpone their fight for national independence and against miserable living and working conditions in the name of a "wartime emergency." Sugar workers in the island's fields and mills waged strike battles for higher wages and decent working conditions. Puerto Rican independence fighters were a special target of the FBI during the war. Several years earlier, in 1936, Pedro Albizu Campos, the central leader of the Puerto Rican Nationalist Party, had been railroaded to a federal prison in Atlanta on charges of conspiracy to overthrow the government and "inciting rebellion" against the United States. When Washington entered the war, the US government offered to free Albizu Campos and some sixty other imprisoned Nationalists if they would agree to suspend all proindependence activity during the war. The Puerto Rican patriots unanimously refused. The Nationalist Party voted to reject conscription into the US Army, since "the United States holds Puerto Rico under a military, illegal government." Washington prosecuted a number of Nationalist Party members for draft evasion, including its former secretary-general, Julio Pinto Gandía. In a June 1945 interview with the *Militant*, Gandía explained:

> I do not evade anything. I simply refuse to fight as a slave of an imperialist power. I will fight as much as is needed, but only for the freedom and independence of my people. I know there are many young men from Puerto Rico in the US army. . . . They think they are fighting for freedom and democracy. But they will learn . . . that kind of fight begins at home.

In Canada, Washington's imperialist partner to the north, opposition to the war and conscription ran deep among the people of another oppressed nation denied its right to independence—the Québécois. In a 1942 Canadian government referendum on instituting a draft, 80 percent of the Québécois voted no. Refusal to register or serve in the armed forces occurred on a massive scale in Quebec. The Canadian government, too, interned and expropriated its west coast Japanese population. Political organizations that opposed Canadian entry into the war, such as the Socialist Workers League, predecessor to today's Revolutionary Workers League, were banned.

Target: Labor movement

The crusade to root out "subversives" in the name of the war for democracy reached far into the working-class movement. The Democratic and Republican parties mouthed support for constitutional freedoms. But the capitalist parties and their government appointees approved the steady expansion of the power of the executive branch to act—publicly when possible, covertly when necessary—to restrict the ground covered by the Bill of Rights.

At the end of the 1930s, war preparations were increasingly being used as a justification to restrict democracy and labor rights. The overriding question facing the labor movement became what attitude to take toward the militarization drive of the ruling class.

There was significant sentiment among working people against another imperialist war, and antiwar forces in the labor movement won a sympathetic hearing from many unionists. There was also widespread sympathy for revolutionary struggles in the colonial countries for independence and self-determination. The coming to power of fascism in Germany and the crushing of the German workers' movement reinforced the determination of millions of workers in the United States to strengthen their class organizations, the unions, as weapons in defense of the working class and its allies.

The attitude of class-struggle forces in the unions was well put in a resolution adopted in 1938 by the Minneapolis Central Labor Union. The adoption of this position was the result of an antiwar campaign spearheaded by Teamster Local 544 in Minneapolis, which had prepared the expansion of Teamster power in the Midwest with its victory over the employers in 1934, opening the door to transforming Minneapolis into a union stronghold. The leadership of Local 544 included leaders of the communist forces who in 1938 initiated the formation of the Socialist Workers Party.

"Be it resolved," said the Minneapolis labor body:

> 1. That the Central Labor Union of Minneapolis, voicing the determination of fifty thousand trade unionists, declares its unalterable opposition to all war preparations and military budgets, and any and all bills in which they are embodied, and stigmatizes the war being prepared as a war of imperialist conquest, and declares its firm opposition to any war launched by the Government;
> 2. That we demand that all war funds now proposed for the military budget and naval expansion be transferred immediately to the relief of the unemployed;
> 3. That we demand the immediate withdrawal of any and all armed forces of the United States from the Far East, since it is only Big Business and not Labor that has any interests there to protect;
> 4. That we assert militant Labor's determination to

support . . . the brave Chinese people in their fight for independence against the Japanese invaders and all other foreign exploiters; and

5. That we shall join with all other forces in the labor movement who share our views for the purpose of consolidating the strongest possible movement of resistance to war and to the war-mongers.

As Roosevelt's New Deal was revealed to be also a war deal, the labor movement as a whole began a political retreat. By the latter half of 1937, the momentum of the CIO's rise was largely spent. There were still important strikes, including in auto, coal, and steel, but these were largely rearguard actions. Bureaucratic control of the unions was becoming tightened in both the CIO and the AFL. With the entry of the US government into the war, top union officials—with the notable exception of a grouping around John L. Lewis of the United Mine Workers union—were accepting Roosevelt's insistence that the interests of union members had to be subordinated to "national unity." The result was a further weakening of the unions, though one that remained largely hidden from the awareness of most union members, given the economic upturn brought about by expanding production for war.

At the same time, the labor movement continued to retreat from its position in the front ranks of the fight for political rights and democratic liberties. During the rise of the CIO, the new union movement had fought to expand labor's right to organize and as a result had widened the latitude for political activity of everyone in this country. But as the union officialdom lined up behind the bipartisan war policies of the ruling class, they were increasingly willing to turn their backs on defense of the Bill of Rights, even when the rights of the unions were directly involved.

The capitalists consequently were largely free to use government power—including the FBI and the courts—to try to isolate, if not silence, those in the labor movement who refused to get in step with the war policies of the Roosevelt administration.

During the 1940 presidential campaign, Roosevelt personally ordered a wiretap on the phone of John L. Lewis, at that time head of the CIO and the miners' union. The president viewed Lewis as a special threat—and a potential troublemaker—because of his decision to break ranks and refuse to support Roosevelt for re-election. The following year, Harry Bridges, leader of the West Coast Longshore union, discovered an FBI tap on his phone. Bridges, who was fighting government moves to deport him on political grounds, made the wiretap public.

Attorney General Biddle later recounted the White House meeting that took place following public protests against the violation of Bridges's constitutional rights. "When all this came out in the newspapers," Biddle wrote, "I could not resist suggesting to [FBI director J. Edgar] Hoover that he tell the story of the unfortunate tap directly to the President. We went over to the White House together. F.D.R. was delighted; and with one of his great grins, intent on every word, slapped Hoover on the back when he had finished. 'By God, Edgar, that's the first time you've been caught with your pants down!' The two men liked and understood each other."[4] The snapshot is revealing. The liberal president, the equally liberal attorney general, and the director of the FBI share a hearty laugh over the subversion of the Bill of Rights.

Nor was this an isolated incident. In 1937, the US Supreme Court had ruled that a federal law prohibiting wiretaps applied to the FBI. In 1940, however, Roosevelt secretly instructed the Justice Department to ignore the court's ruling:

> I am convinced that the Supreme Court never intended any dictum in the particular case which it decided to apply to grave matters involving the defense of the nation.... You are, therefore, authorized and directed in such cases as you may approve, after investigation of the need in each case, to authorize the necessary investigating agents that they are at liberty to secure information by listening devices directed to the conversation or other communications of *persons suspected of subversive activities* against the Government of the United States, including suspected spies. (Emphasis added.)

Around the same time, the FBI expanded its army of informers and provocateurs in the labor and Black movements. FBI field offices were instructed to recruit or place informers in every plant engaged in war production—most of the large factories in the country. By the end of 1942, there were nearly 24,000 FBI stool pigeons reporting on union and political activities in almost 4,000 factories, mines, and mills.

Frame-up in Minneapolis

In 1941 the Roosevelt administration, working in concert with the top International officials of the Teamsters, moved against the class-struggle leadership of the Minneapolis Teamsters. This leadership had refused to retreat from its position that labor must organize itself and set its priorities independent of the needs and prerogatives of the capitalist government and political parties. It continued to argue for the formation of a labor party based on the unions. It defended the colonial freedom struggle and championed the fight for the rights of oppressed nationalities in the United States. And it fought every move to sap the power of the labor movement by bringing unions under the control of government agencies.

The legal centerpiece of the Roosevelt administration's antilabor offensive was the use for the first time of the Smith Act, which had been adopted in 1940. For the first time in the United States since the Alien and Sedition Acts of 1798, this gag law made the *expression of ideas* a crime.

In June 1941, FBI agents and US marshals raided the branch offices of the Socialist Workers Party in St. Paul and Minneapolis. They hauled away cartons of communist literature from the bookstores and libraries on the premises.

In Washington, D.C., Attorney General Biddle himself announced the plans for prosecution. "The principal Socialist Workers Party leaders against whom prosecution is being brought are also leaders of Local 544-CIO in Minneapolis," he told the press. "The prosecution is brought under the criminal code of the United States against persons who have been engaged in criminal seditious activities, and who are leaders of the Socialist Workers Party and have gained control of a legitimate labor union to use it for illegitimate purposes." Biddle's harangues against editors of Black papers provide a pretty good idea of the broad scope the attorney general gave to the term "seditious activities." From the standpoint of the government, any union activity dissenting from the drive toward entry into the war was illegitimate.

The government had three objectives in the crackdown on the Teamster local and the SWP.

First, it aimed to purge the labor movement of those who would not go along with imperialist war goals and militarization of the country and to intimidate into silence others, inside and outside the unions.

Second, the government wanted to erase the stronghold of union power and democracy represented by the Minneapolis Teamsters. The leadership of that union was inspiring emulation of class-struggle methods throughout the Midwest and educating workers in the need for socially conscious labor action and political independence from the capitalist parties. Although these leaders represented a minority point of view in the labor movement, that could change. The fight they were waging could become a rallying point to draw together significant forces in the unions, among the unemployed and unorganized, among Blacks, and among working farmers.

Third, the government sought to push the SWP in the direction of going underground. It wanted to force the party to give up some of its public activities and to concede that it must function at least in part illegally. The rulers' goal was to restrict the space for working-class politics.

The relationship of class forces imposed by the labor movement's retreat allowed the capitalist government a good measure of success in its first and second objectives. But it totally failed in driving the SWP underground. One of the party's first responses to the indictments was to nominate James P. Cannon, its national secretary and one of those facing trial, for mayor of New York City. The SWP launched a vigorous petition campaign to win Cannon a spot on the ballot. The party also initiated a nationwide defense effort that continued until the last of the defendants was released from prison. Throughout this fight, the SWP forcefully asserted its constitutional right to carry out political activity. It published and distributed Marxist literature. It participated in and helped to advance the activities of the unions, the NAACP, and other organizations. SWP members explained communist ideas to fellow GIs, fought together with them against race discrimination in the armed forces and other abuses of citizen-soldiers, and took advantage of every opportunity to present the views of the party.

A central issue in the Minneapolis trial was the SWP's opposition to any policy of subordinating the interests of unionists, Blacks, GIs, farmers, or other working people to the profits and power of the exploiters, who called for "national unity" in wartime to silence opposition to their policies. In time of war, the SWP explained, the struggle for the independence of the trade unions from the capitalist state and the fight for trade union democracy become even more critical.

SWP leaders turned the courtroom into a platform from which to explain the party's views on the war. They explained that the Second World War was really three wars in one.

First, it was a war to defend the Soviet Union, the first—and at that time the only—workers' state, against imperialist efforts spearheaded by Germany's rulers to overturn it and restore capitalist rule. In this conflict the workers' movement throughout the world stood with the Soviet workers' state.

Second, it was a war for national liberation, especially in Asia. The Chinese, Indian, Vietnamese, and other colonial peoples were waging massive struggles against imperialist occupation and domination, taking advantage of the conflict between the world imperialist powers to push for their own freedom. In this war all of progressive humanity stood with the colonial peoples against their imperialist overlords.

Third, it was a war among imperialist rivals for domination of the world. In this conflict, the capitalist rulers of the United States and those of its allies sought to enlist the political support of working people by presenting their goals as the defeat of fascism and defense of democracy. But, as SWP leader James P. Cannon explained from the witness stand, US working people could combat fascism only by strengthening their own organizations not by subordinating their struggle to support for the imperialist government, in wartime or not. Cannon was asked:

> What is the party's position on the claim that the war against Hitler is a war of democracy against fascism?

ANSWER: We say that it is a subterfuge, that the conflict between American imperialism and German imperialism is for the domination of the world. It is absolutely true that Hitler wants to dominate the world, but we think it is equally true that the ruling group of American capitalists has the same idea, and we are not in favor of either of them.

We do not think that the Sixty Families who own America want to wage this war for some sacred principle of democracy. We think they are the greatest enemies of democracy here at home. We think they would only use the opportunity of a war to eliminate all civil liberties at home, to get the best imitation of fascism they can possibly get.[5]

The government's case at the trial consisted largely of testimony from FBI stool pigeons and other opponents of the elected leadership of Teamster Local 544, together with evidence such as copies of the *Communist Manifesto* and other books and pamphlets by Marx, Engels, Lenin, and Trotsky that had been seized from bookstore shelves.

A jury returned convictions against eighteen of the twenty-eight defendants on one count of the indictment, finding them guilty of a conspiracy to "advise and teach the duty, necessity, desirability and propriety of overthrowing and destroying the Government of the United States by force and violence...." Sentencing took place on December 8, 1941, the day after the Japanese forces attacked the main naval base in the US colony of Hawaii, and the day Congress voted a formal declaration of war. Twelve of the defendants received sentences of sixteen months in federal prison, and six were sentenced to one year.

Opponents of this political persecution joined together to organize the Civil Rights Defense Committee (CRDC).

The guilty verdict brought forth a round of protests from union locals and central labor bodies speaking for more than five million union members. Union bodies contributed money to the CRDC to pay for legal appeals and help spread the word about the case. Support came from NAACP chapters around the country. W.E.B. Du Bois, the historian and Black rights leader, declared his solidarity with the Smith Act defendants. Adam Clayton Powell, then a member of the New York City Council and a prominent figure in the Black community, declared: "Whenever the civil liberties of any American or any American group are threatened, then the civil liberties of all are in danger, and this is the issue in Minneapolis." The American Civil Liberties Union announced its support for the appeal, warning that the Smith Act is a "dangerous weapon against civil rights of labor and radicals of all varieties."

Support for the defense effort was not universal in the working-class movement, however. Most AFL and CIO officials remained silent; some even publicly supported the prosecution.

A treacherous stand was taken by the Stalinized Communist Party, which gave political support to the Roosevelt administration and its appeals for "national unity." In the union movement, the CP was among the most fervent backers of the no-strike pledge agreed to by most of the top labor officialdom for the duration of the war. When the United Mine Workers went on strike in 1943, the CP's *Daily Worker* openly opposed it and called for the "[John L.] Lewis line" of defying the no-strike pledge to be "utterly defeated." In the Black movement, the CP opposed the Double V campaign on the grounds that too much emphasis on the fight against race discrimination in the army and in the war plants would disrupt "national unity." The CP also supported the internment of Japanese Americans, suspended from the party its Japanese American members, and urged these former members not to resist their own internment.[6]

Consistent with these positions, the Communist Party actively supported the prosecution of the Minneapolis defendants. The *Daily Worker* branded those who supported the Civil Rights Defense Committee as "tools" being used by "Hitler agents."

When the guilty verdicts were returned, the *Daily Worker* published a major article on December 19 by Carl Winter headlined "Minneapolis Trial Shows Labor Wary of Trotzkyites." Winter argued that no support should be given to the Minneapolis defendants because they were not a legitimate part of the labor movement. If the federal prosecutors deserve criticism, Winter said, it was for falsely portraying the SWP leaders as revolutionary communists rather than agents of Hitler. He went on:

> Their fifth column service to Hitlerism through spreading disunity in labor's ranks, trying to undermine and weaken the all-out defense effort, and viciously inciting against the Soviet Union received little attention. Instead, the "radical" mask under which all this was carried on was taken at face value by the prosecution and the Trotzkyite pretense of being a militant working-class organization was used to obtain the first conviction under the reactionary Smith Act.
>
> While the trial has aroused a vigilance in Minnesota labor and progressive circles against the danger of misuse of this precedent, there has been a general refusal to accept the evaluation of the Trotzkyites as "radicals," as painted by the prosecution, instead of their known worth as servants of reaction. Significantly, there have been no local unions to date with the possible exception of those

under their control to come forward in joining the Trotzkyites in their appeal in this case....

If the federal prosecution of the Trotzkyites failed to fully reveal their fifth column character, current events and the growing alertness of the American people will soon contribute to pulling the fangs of these copperheads in labor's ranks.

It is easy to see how damaging this position was to the working-class movement and to the fight against imperialism. But it is not as simple to understand why so many CP leaders and members believed it to be the right position, just as they deeply believed that a ban on strikes during the war was essential, and that the fight for civil rights for Blacks had to be put on the back burner.

The recent outpouring of books and articles examining the history of the US Communist Party, both by academic historians and by former CP members, sheds little light on this question. Anticommunist liberal and social democratic writers argue that CP leaders simply took orders from Moscow and that the membership was either duped or corrupted into going along with positions that they did not understand or believe in. Those more sympathetic to the CP of the past try to make an often sentimental case that the party's positions on world political developments were largely irrelevant to the day-to-day political work of the rank-and-file. For its part, the Communist Party today disavows some of the most extreme formulations from the World War II period, dismissing them as excesses for which a single individual, CP general secretary Earl Browder, was responsible. (Browder was dumped without ceremony from the CP leadership in July 1945 on instructions from the Soviet party leadership.)

All these explanations are false. None explains why tens

"A contradiction was growing between what the US ruling class was compelled to do against its class enemies at home and abroad, and what it could openly proclaim as its goals and methods."

FLAX HERMES/MILITANT

GLEN CAMPBELL/MILITANT

In the early 1970s, the "Watergate" revelations of wiretapping and burglary by Nixon administration against its capitalist political opponents put spotlight on secret FBI, CIA, and other political police operations. The Socialist Workers Party filed a lawsuit in 1973 against government spying and disruption of working-class organizations.

ABOVE: New York, July 1973, news conference announcing suit by SWP. From right: Linda Jenness, party's 1972 candidate for US president; constitutional attorney Leonard Boudin; Andrew Pulley, SWP candidate for vice-president.

INSET: Picket against FBI director Clarence Kelley in Cleveland, September 1976.

"As Cointelpro and other FBI operations became known, it was clear the capitalist government's use of these methods against class enemies abroad was an extension of its war against class enemies at home."

MARK SATINOFF/MILITANT

STUART KIEHL/MILITANT

US government carried out disruption and harassment of Black rights, women's liberation, antiwar, and communist organizations.

TOP: November 1971 march in Washington, DC, in support of a woman's right to choose abortion.

BOTTOM: May 1971 demonstration in New York demanding immediate withdrawal of US troops from Vietnam.

ELI FINER/MILITANT

ABOVE: Malcolm X (right) speaks at Militant Labor Forum, New York, January 1965. Clifton DeBerry (left), 1964 Socialist Workers Party candidate for US president, chaired meeting.

INSET: FBI document dated May 1965 tells undercover agents to carry out disruption tactics that could be used "to drive a wedge between the followers of Malcolm X and the SWP."

"By the mid-1930s a vast social movement was on the rise in the mines, mills, and factories. The bosses knew that views defended by respected working-class fighters who were communists could rapidly gain support."

TOP: St. Louis, May 1932. Jobless World War I veterans head to Washington, DC, demanding federal "Soldiers' Bonus." The "Bonus March" was one of first mass actions by working people during Great Depression.

BOTTOM: Teamsters defend themselves against police assault during 1934 strike in Minneapolis. Five-week action established the union throughout city's trucking industry and opened way to organization of over-the-road truckers and other workers across Midwest.

MINNESOTA HISTORICAL SOCIETY

WALTER P. REUTHER LABOR LIBRARY

TOP: Grant County, Minnesota, 1935. March by Farmers Holiday Association, which fought farm foreclosures and organized to withhold produce from market to win higher payments from capitalist food merchants.
MIDDLE: FBI director J. Edgar Hoover (to right of flag) at White House in May 1934, as President Franklin Roosevelt signs laws increasing federal police powers for use against labor movement.
BOTTOM: January 1937 sit-in strike at General Motors, Flint, Michigan, one of 250 factory occupations that year by auto workers and others. Striking workers won recognition of United Auto Workers on industrial-union basis.

"In 1941 federal prosecutors moved against the Minneapolis Teamsters leadership and Socialist Workers Party. They used for the first time the Smith Act, a gag law that made the expression of ideas a crime."

MILITANT

Eighteen leaders of Local 544-CIO and Socialist Workers Party were indicted in 1941 and imprisoned two years later on frame-up charges of "conspiracy to advocate the overthrow of the US government by force and violence." US rulers aimed to purge union of those opposing imperialist war goals, break stronghold of union power in Minneapolis, and force SWP to give up public activities.

FACING PAGE, RIGHT: FBI raids SWP headquarters in Minneapolis, June 1941, seizing boxes of books, pamphlets, and newspapers.

FACING PAGE, LEFT: 1941 issues of the *Militant* and *Industrial Organizer*, newspaper of Local 544-CIO, campaign against Roosevelt administration's antilabor frame-up.

ABOVE: Minneapolis, December 31, 1943. Leaders of SWP and Local 544-CIO march to federal courthouse to begin sentences of up to sixteen months. At front are, from left, V.R. Dunne, James P. Cannon, and Carl Skoglund.

"During World War II many working people refused to halt fight against miserable living and job conditions in name of 'wartime emergency.'"

ABOVE: Members of United Mine Workers union on strike in Ohio, May 1943. In response to government strike-breaking threats, miners replied, "You can't mine coal with bayonets."

In 1941 Black rights organizations called for March on Washington to demand end to segregation in war industries and armed forces. Leaders, under government pressure, called off Washington march but organized mass rallies in 1942 and 1943 in New York, Chicago, Detroit, and elsewhere.

BOTTOM: 1941 pamphlet by Pioneer Press, forerunner of Pathfinder, supporting March on Washington movement; poster publicizing its demands.

ABOVE: Yabucoa, Puerto Rico, January 1942. Striking sugar workers ignored claim they were "sabotaging national defense" and won 20 percent pay increase across island.

In 1936 Washington framed and jailed Puerto Rican Nationalist Party leader Pedro Albizu Campos and sixty others on charges of "conspiracy" to overthrow government. During World War II, the jailed militants refused US offer to free them if they suspended pro-independence activity and backed military conscription.

INSET: Albizu Campos addresses sugar strikers in earlier battle, January 1934.

BOTTOM: Anti-conscription action in Quebec, November 1944, after 16,000 draftees across Canada were ordered to report for duty overseas.

"What came to be known as the McCarthy era is often presented as a sharp break from the Roosevelt years. In fact, it was an extension of the assault on constitutional liberties that administration had begun."

In 1949, eleven Communist Party leaders were indicted and jailed for violating the Smith Act, the same thought-control law used against SWP and Teamster leaders eight years earlier. CP had backed federal prosecution of defendants in Minneapolis trial.

ABOVE: October 1949 protest in Philadelphia, two weeks before trial of the CP leaders opened in New York. **INSET:** *Militant* headline reports guilty verdict; the socialist weekly had campaigned, since June 1949 indictment, for a united defense of CP frame-up victims.

LIBRARY OF CONGRESS

MILITANT

Julius and Ethel Rosenberg were arrested in 1950, tried and convicted for "conspiracy" to commit espionage in 1951, and executed in June 1953. The CP leadership organized no defense campaign for the Rosenbergs, apparently hoping to insulate party against charges that some in its ranks had spied for Soviet Union.

ABOVE: Demonstrators in New York, bound for protest in Washington, DC, June 18, 1953. Rosenbergs were executed next day. **INSET:** Ethel and Julius Rosenberg, March 1951.

James Kutcher, legless World War II veteran and Socialist Workers Party member fired from government job in 1948 "loyalty" purge, won back his job after eight-year fight supported by hundreds of unions and other organizations across US.

BELOW: Kutcher seeks backing at CIO convention in Ohio, November 1949.

In mid-1950s, the FBI opened "Cointelpro" (counterintelligence) operations against the Communist Party, Black groups, and Socialist Workers Party in order to "infiltrate, penetrate, disorganize, and disrupt" them, in the words of J. Edgar Hoover.

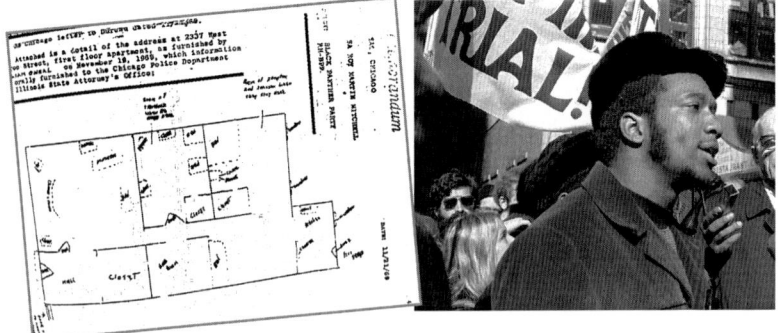

ABOVE: *The Worker*, newspaper of Communist Party, July 1964. FBI fabricated material to finger William Albertson, chair of New York CP, as informer. CP leadership fell into trap and publicly expelled him. Subsequently, FBI documents boasting of "snitch jacket" operation were released.

Black Panthers leaders Fred Hampton and Mark Clark were killed in 1969 in a nighttime police raid on a Chicago apartment. **BELOW, RIGHT:** Hampton speaking at rally in Chicago, October 1969. Hampton's bodyguard, an FBI informer, provided cops with apartment floor plan (below left).

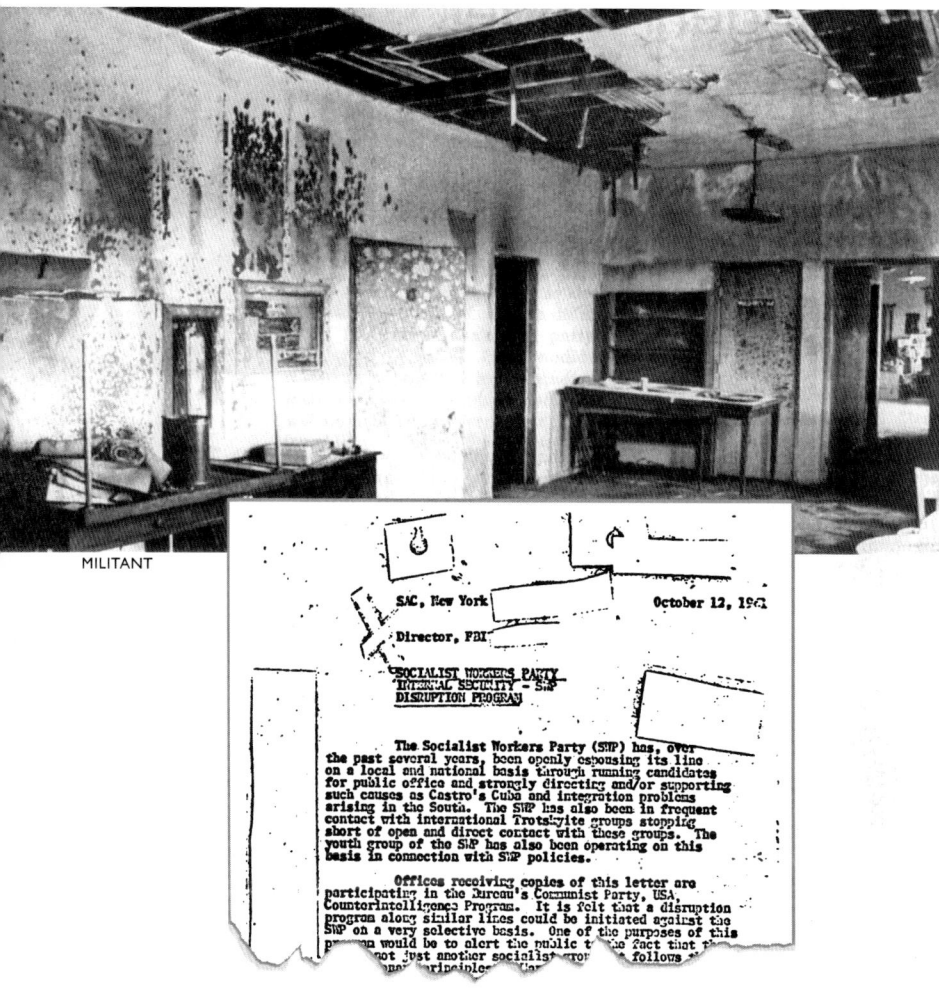

FBI launched a "Socialist Workers Party Disruption Program." One of the reasons given was party's support to Cuban Revolution.

ABOVE: Los Angeles, May 1970. SWP headquarters after firebombing by counterrevolutionary Cuban paramilitary squad, one of groups with long history of working closely with FBI and CIA. The attack, carried out at midday while four people were inside, was the sixth against Los Angeles SWP in two years. **BELOW:** October 1961 FBI document outlining "Disruption Program" against the party.

"The SWP lawsuit was an unprecedented political initiative. Communist workers—along with fellow unionists, farmers, and others—were plaintiffs. Government agencies and officials were defendants. Not the other way around."—*From the introduction*

Suit went to trial in April 1981. **ABOVE:** Government attorney Edward G. Williams (back row, right), Judge Thomas Griesa (seated at bench), SWP leader Farrell Dobbs (testifying), SWP attorney Margaret Winter (right).

"Revolution," said Dobbs, "is a cumulative process of the education and organization of the working class to act in its own behalf. That's the only way a social transformation can be brought about."

DRAWINGS BY DIANE JACOBS/MILITANT

TOP: SWP national secretary Jack Barnes explained that the party fights for a workers and farmers government, "a socialist soviet democracy in which working people run the country and expand the involvement of the majority of the population in the economy and politics of the country." Cuban Revolution, he said, "made greatest attempt to do this since the Bolshevik-led revolution in Russia in 1917."

BOTTOM LEFT: Robert Keuch, associate deputy attorney general in Carter administration. Keuch told court FBI's operations against SWP had been authorized by Franklin Roosevelt, who had "inherent power" as president to "protect our form of government."

BOTTOM RIGHT: Herbert Brownell, attorney general in Eisenhower administration, argued that 1956 "presidential directive" was sufficient legal basis for FBI "Cointelpro" covert operations.

"Rights won by Socialist Workers Party opened broader space for politics by working people seeking to defend themselves and advance their interests."

ABOVE: Headlines across US, from *New York Times* to *Muhammad Speaks*, highlighted exposure of FBI operations by SWP suit. *New York Daily News* editorial, August 1986, welcomes federal court ruling. *New York Times* editorial, earlier in suit, October 1975, calls for halt to FBI spying on SWP and others.

Over course of struggle, thousands of unionists, students, artists, civil libertarians, and others across the US lent support to Political Rights Defense Fund (PRDF), which mobilized support for SWP suit.

ABOVE: Morton Sobell (center), witch-hunt victim convicted together with Rosenbergs but on lesser charges, speaks at June 1981 New York rally of 700 in support of suit. Next to him are SWP attorney Margaret Winter (left) and literary critic Annette Rubinstein. Other speakers included comedian and civil rights fighter Dick Gregory and Ernesto Joffre, president of Amalgamated Clothing and Textile Workers Local 169.

BELOW: March 1988 press conference in New York registers victory against federal government, which had announced it would not appeal court decision barring FBI spying on SWP. From left: SWP national secretary Jack Barnes; Leonard Boudin, attorney for SWP; and PRDF director John Studer.

"The capitalist rulers will not prevent Mark Curtis from continuing to be the person he is today, fighting for the same things, holding the same convictions, saying them openly to the world."
—*Jack Barnes, September 1988*

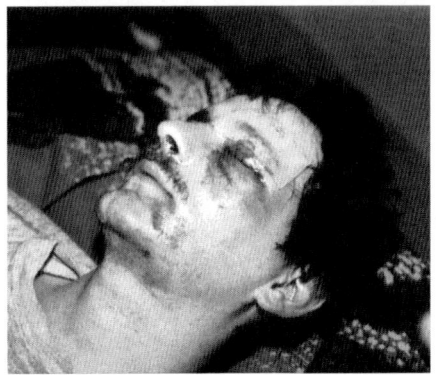

STU SINGER/MILITANT

PHIL NORRIS/MILITANT

STU SINGER/MILITANT

Mark Curtis, packinghouse worker, union militant, and member of SWP, was arrested and beaten by police in Des Moines, Iowa, March 1988. He was convicted and sentenced to 25 years on frame-up charges of attempted rape and burglary. An eight-year battle won his release on parole. Curtis's arrest and beating came just days after SWP won final round in suit against FBI.

TOP LEFT: Mark Curtis after beating by cops. **TOP RIGHT:** Before frame-up, at May 1987 rally for striking packinghouse workers, Sioux Falls, South Dakota. **BOTTOM:** With FBI spy files on his activity against US military intervention in Central America.

TOP: Speakers at rally for Curtis in Des Moines, September 1988, just before trial opened. Jack Barnes, SWP national secretary, speaking; (from left) Mark Curtis; defense committee organizers Ellen Whitt, Nan Bailey; Hazel Zimmerman, treasurer of committee.

In August 1988 a victory was won in another defense campaign. US government dropped its decade-long effort to deport Héctor Marroquín, Mexican-born member of SWP and plaintiff in party's lawsuit, and granted him permanent residency.

BOTTOM: Marroquín addressing July 1983 convention of National Education Association. NEA, largest teachers union in US, reaffirmed support to Marroquín's fight against deportation.

"Five Cuban revolutionists—arrested in 1998 FBI raids—have conducted themselves from behind bars with pride and dignity as they defend their revolutionary principles and rebut charges fabricated by US authorities."

—*From the introduction*

ABOVE, FROM LEFT: Gerardo Hernández, Ramón Labañino, Antonio Guerrero. **BELOW:** Fernando González (left), René González.

The Cuban Five, as they are known to millions worldwide, were arrested and framed by Washington on false espionage and other "conspiracy" charges. They were gathering information on plans of murderous Cuban American paramilitary outfits in Florida, in order to prevent future deadly attacks against Cuba and supporters of the revolution. They proudly say they would do the same again.

Gerardo, Ramón, and Antonio remain behind bars.

of thousands of working people who considered themselves dedicated communist fighters argued for and believed in the party's political positions. They were not fools, and they were not cowards. Nor, by and large, were they simply careerists or opportunists.

Revolutionary-minded working-class fighters who joined the CP understood that the Soviet workers' state had to be defended against imperialism by the working-class movement everywhere. They recognized in the Soviet Union an historic conquest of the world working class. But they were taught in the CP that this meant that the conjunctural needs of the Soviet government, as defined by the Stalin regime, coincided with how best to advance the interests of the working class in the United States and worldwide. Thus, all other considerations had to be subordinated to the Soviet government's current policies. The main positions of the CP in the United States, as elsewhere, were dictated in accordance with the frequently shifting requirements of Stalin's diplomacy. The members of the Communist Party believed this was in the interests of the US and international working class and believed it deeply. Those who did not share this perspective did not stay in the party very long.[7]

Following the Seventh Congress of the Communist International in August 1935, the US Communist Party turned toward increasingly open political support for the Roosevelt administration and the New Deal. This was in accord with Stalin's new Popular Front line, which put forward—as the only road to defeat German fascism and its growing military threat to the Soviet Union—the subordination of independent working-class politics to an alliance with bourgeois governments and liberal capitalist parties in the imperialist countries. In the CIO, the CP actively opposed motion toward a labor party based on the unions that would challenge *both* capitalist parties. The CP's 1936 presidential campaign was waged around the slogan of defeating Roosevelt's Republican Party challenger "at all costs."

When Stalin signed a nonaggression pact with Hitler in August 1939, however, Communist Party members immediately became opponents of both Roosevelt and his militarization policy. Then, after Hitler tore up the nonaggression pact and invaded the Soviet Union in June 1941, CP members immediately once again became ardent supporters of Roosevelt and campaigners for war by the United States against Germany and Japan. They did not have to be "ordered" by Moscow to reverse their line over night. They *believed* it was correct to do so, because it served the Soviet Union's needs, as Stalin defined them and CP members understood them.

Nowhere was this more striking than in the position of the CP on the colonial revolution. With the wartime military alliance between the United States, Britain, and the Soviet Union, the struggles for independence in the colonies and semicolonies of the Allied imperialist powers became, in the CP's view, an obstacle to the fight against fascism. The toilers of Latin America were told to unite with US imperialism and its local henchmen.

In Cuba, formally an independent republic but in reality a US semicolony, the Stalinists proclaimed themselves "the most tenacious defenders of the unity of our country with the United States." The leadership of the Communist Party posed the question directly: "Why isn't the struggle against imperialism put first?" And it answered: "the principal task of all peoples of the world today is to defeat Nazism; every other interest must be subordinated to this task." Blas Roca, then central leader of the party, went so far as to quote with approval the assertion of Sumner

Welles, US ambassador to Cuba, that the "imperialist era has ended."

The Cuban Stalinists likewise sought to deepen class collaboration with the Cuban capitalists and landlords. (In line with this, the party dropped the name "Communist" in 1944 and became the Popular Socialist Party.) In 1945 Blas Roca, in a speech to union officials on "Collaboration Between Workers and Employers," criticized workers who "do not understand the new conditions and still cling to the concepts which, while formerly correct, today no longer correspond to reality."

Roca added that in the past, Social Democrats and reformists called for "class collaboration with no concrete goal because they could not admit that its goal was to preserve capitalism." What the PSP called for, however, was "national unity, one of the highest forms of class collaboration at this time, with a concrete goal—defeat Hitlerism, guarantee peace, and promote national liberation." The PSP campaigned against strikes, for universal conscription, and for sending Cuban troops to fight in the imperialist war.

With the Popular Front turn of the Communist International, the Cuban party affirmed its new stance toward proimperialist dictator Colonel Fulgencio Batista. "We have concluded that Batista is taking positions that favor a democratic, popular, and progressive policy," said Roca at the party's Third National Assembly in January 1939. "Based on his assessment, we have decided to adopt a positive stance toward him." During the war, the party strengthened its backing for Batista, and he appointed two PSP leaders to his cabinet in 1943–44.[8]

Throughout Latin America, Communist parties followed similar lines. In a recent interview, Tomás Borge, a leader of the Sandinista National Liberation Front and Nicaragua's Minister of the Interior, reviewed the obstacles created by this policy to the development of the working-class movement in that country and elsewhere:

> The workers' movement of Nicaragua emerged as a political organization May 1, 1944, in the midst of the World War and at a time when "Browderism" was making deep inroads in this continent. Earl Browder, general secretary of the Communist Party of the United States, held the view that the antagonistic contradiction between the bourgeoisie and the working class had disappeared. This concept was developed by a party that came onto the scene prior to the Nicaraguan Socialist Party, the Peoples Vanguard Party of Costa Rica.
>
> Thus, a notion that held great influence was the idea that any government that had declared war on fascism had to be supported to the utmost. The workers' movement in Nicaragua emerged with the deviation, one shared by other politically organized workers' movements in Latin America, that local dictators should be supported.
>
> The Nicaraguan Socialist Party emerged on the scene supporting the Somoza dictatorship. That's why Marxism in Nicaragua has no history.
>
> The history of Marxism in Nicaragua began in 1944 and it is a sad history; in other words, properly speaking, it is not even the history of Marxism. Marxism, which is a revolutionary theory, cannot be tarnished by sadness.
>
> In the concrete case of Nicaragua, those who in those days called themselves Marxists were mired in a policy of class collaboration, of support to the bourgeoisie and to US imperialism, which, as we know, was at that time at war with fascism. I don't want to go back over who was historically responsible for this; I don't want to point to those who were guilty. This was, objectively, the history, regardless of the sins and the sinners.[9]

To those who did not understand the Stalinist political framework in which members of the Communist parties had been educated, the sudden switches by these parties seemed irrational. But to those trained in the school of Stalinism, any other course would have been unthinkable. Loyal CP members followed, without a great deal of difficulty, the reversals of line required by Moscow's shifting relations with various imperialist powers. What mattered to them was the defense of the Soviet Union as they understood it.

Those who broke from this position had no reason to stay in the Communist Party, and they did not. This explains why thousands, perhaps tens of thousands, of members and supporters of the US Communist Party who stuck through the twists and turns of its policies in the 1930s and 1940s, and through the worst days of the McCarthyite reaction in the 1950s, broke definitively from the CP when Khrushchev's speech at the twentieth congress of the Soviet Communist Party in 1956 revealed some of Stalin's crimes against the Soviet workers' state and its vanguard. The basis of their whole world outlook appeared to have shattered overnight.

Over time, this Stalinist course corroded all communist principles. The CP was no longer guided by how the working class and its allies in the United States and worldwide could best advance along their historic line of march in the struggle against imperialist exploitation and oppression. Instead of recognizing the Soviet Union as a bastion to aid the world revolution, the Stalinists subordinated the struggles of workers and farmers to the perceived diplomatic needs of the Soviet government.

Communist Party members themselves rationalized this course based on their belief that, whatever the political price, the course of the Stalin regime did serve the long-term interests of the world revolution. But many other working people could not be easily convinced. So the real reasons for positions taken by the CP on a strike, a fight for Black rights, or a presidential election campaign were often no longer identical to the "good" reasons given to the workers and their allies.

Along with this came the introduction of the idea, which became widespread in the Popular Front era, that it was necessary and desirable to have members of the party who were not known as Communists even to their fellow workers and political collaborators. That way it was easier to help the liberals, without running the risk of embarrassing them. It became acceptable to lie to the working class about political positions—in the name of defending the Soviet Union.

A necessary by-product of this Stalinist course was the superfactionalism introduced by the CP into the workers' movement. The tradition of working-class solidarity in the face of government attack despite political differences was consciously broken by the CP. Those who disagreed with Communist Party positions were branded enemies of the Soviet Union, then tools or conscious agents of Hitler. Communists who proposed an alternative to Stalin's course in the Soviet Union, including Leon Trotsky and other opposition forces in the Soviet CP and the Communist International, were slandered and killed by Stalin's murder machine.

It was in line with this overall course that the US Communist Party gave backing to the government's jailing of SWP leaders under the Smith Act. No other course was possible for the CP even to consider.

McCarthy-era witch hunt

With the defeat of Germany and Japan and the new rise of revolutionary struggles set in motion by the world war, Washington quickly moved to end the wartime alliance with Moscow. It was soon replaced by the cold war. The US government and its British and French allies intensified their efforts to stop the advance of colonial revolts in Asia and Africa and the establishment of workers' and farmers' regimes in countries occupied by the Red Army following its smashing of the Third Reich. With the victory of the Chinese revolution in 1949 and the outbreak of the Korean War the following year, the confrontation sharpened between the imperialist powers on the one hand and the colonial revolution and the workers' states on the other.

In the United States the economic boom (which had begun during World War II, brought about by massive war spending) was the new framework in which the struggle between labor and capital was taking place. In the unions, the bureaucracy further consolidated its hold. The strength of the labor movement continued to erode, although this was difficult for many union members to recognize since labor was still wresting wage gains despite the class-collaborationist methods and policies of the officialdom. The labor bureaucracy and its supporters focused attention on the steady, if slow, improvement in real wages for those sections of the work force already organized in the strongest unions. At the same time, they went along with policies that eroded union control over pace and conditions of work and sapped union power by further entangling the labor movement in red tape and restrictive government regulations.

As part of this retreat, the union officialdom refused to wage any battle against the spread of the witch hunt that had begun before World War II. In relation to democratic rights, this postwar period, which came to be known as the McCarthy era, is often presented as a sharp break from the political direction of the Roosevelt administration. Far from a reversal, however, the McCarthy period was an extension of the assault on constitutional liberties that had begun at the end of the 1930s in the name of vigilance against subversives. To their horror and genuine surprise, many who had been willing to keep their mouths shut or even support the government when the FBI went after the Black Muslims or John L. Lewis or the Socialist Workers Party now found themselves targets of the thought-control police.

Within the working-class movement, the strategic orientations of both the Social Democrats and Stalinists were obstacles to an effective fight for democratic rights.

The Socialist Party leaders rejected the perspective of revolutionary struggle by workers and farmers against US capitalism as part of a worldwide fight. Instead they sought to persuade working people to team up with enlightened elements of the US ruling class in defense of "democracy" and against the creation of new workers' and farmers' governments, which would only spread what they condemned as "communist totalitarianism." When SP leaders said "we," they didn't mean the working people of the world but an alliance with a section of the capitalist class. The "they" to be fought against were not the capitalist exploiters but revolutionary democratic struggles in China, Korea, and elsewhere in the colonial and semicolonial world, as well as communists everywhere. With the advent of the cold war, the Social Democrats' course coincided more and more with that of US imperialism, earning them the name "State Department socialists."

While some individual Socialist Party members and leaders took principled stands in defense of victims of the witch hunt, the party's political course undermined the political fight against it. The tradition of the militant working-class movement in this country had been to defend all victims of government repression as a matter of principle. Evidence of "guilt" produced by the government was irrelevant to this class standpoint. During the McCarthy years, the Social Democrats followed an opposite course: arguing that the witch hunt must not victimize the "innocent" and should target only real spies, real communists, real "subversives." Those who could not *prove their innocence* to the satisfaction of these guardians of democracy did not get any support.

The fight against the witch hunt was also hampered by the course of the Communist Party, whose members and supporters bore the brunt of government victimization and harassment. The Stalinist party was by far the largest organization speaking in the name of Marxism in the United States. The CP had already declined some in size because of the political conservatization of the working class resulting from relative postwar prosperity. And it had lost the goodwill of many class-conscious workers due to its extreme factionalism and support for the no-strike pledge and government union busting during the war. But the CP still commanded the political allegiance of hundreds of thousands of workers and could appeal to many more for active collaboration in defense of civil liberties despite political disagreements.

The Communist Party was incapable of mobilizing an effective fight against government repression, however. During the Popular Front period, the CP had oriented toward and loyally served liberal capitalist forces and those in the unions and Black movement who looked to the liberals. With the onset of the cold war, these capitalist forces turned on the CP, as did their lieutenants in the labor movement. Many CP members, as a result, felt they had nowhere to turn in order to counter this new anticommunist offensive by the ruling class. For too long their eyes had been not on the ranks of the labor movement and labor's allies, but on the very forces that were now spearheading the attack on democratic rights.

In 1948 twelve members of the Central Committee of the Communist Party were indicted under the Smith Act. They were charged with conspiring to "teach and advocate the overthrow and destruction of the government of the United States by force and violence"—the very charges used against the Minneapolis defendants seven years earlier. The indictment asserted that this alleged conspiracy had been advanced in three ways: (1) by organizing the Communist Party; (2) by arranging to "publish and circulate, and cause to be circulated, books, articles, magazines, and newspapers advocating the principles of Marxism-Leninism"; and (3) by organizing "schools and classes for the study of the principles of Marxism-Leninism. . . ."

The trial lasted nine months in the federal courthouse at Foley Square in New York City. It concluded with a verdict of guilty against eleven CP leaders. The case against the twelfth, William Z. Foster, had been severed owing to ill health. Ten defendants got the maximum sentence of five years; one received a three-year term. In addition, all the defense attorneys were sentenced to prison terms for "contempt of court" during the trial.

While the Smith Act convictions were on appeal, the legal and political situation worsened. In 1950 Congress adopted the McCarran Act, which required the CP and its members to register with the government. The new law, enacted with bipartisan support, also provided for the setting up of concentration camps where opponents of government policy could be imprisoned without trial during a "national emergency."

In March 1951 Ethel and Julius Rosenberg and Morton Sobell were tried and convicted on frame-up charges and concocted evidence of stealing the "secret" of the atom bomb and giving it to the Soviet Union. On April 5 the Rosenbergs were sentenced to death by electrocution; Sobell was given thirty years. A few months later the US Supreme Court upheld the constitutionality of the Smith Act, rejecting the appeals of the eleven CP defendants.

The intensification of the witch hunt since the end of the 1940s had sparked a debate in the Communist Party leadership over what to do next. A sharp dispute erupted in the leadership over whether the Smith Act defendants, who had been out on bail while their appeals were pending, should turn themselves in or should go into hiding or exile if the Supreme Court ruled against them. Those who favored the latter course argued that fascism was spreading across the country and that the outlawing of the CP was inevitable.

In the end the leadership was unable to reach a decision one way or the other. The upshot was that those defendants who favored going into hiding or exile did so; the others turned themselves in. Whether this was an agreed-upon compromise or the result of a failure to resolve the conflict was not clear to those who were not involved. In any event, when the time came to surrender to federal marshals, four of the eleven defendants did not appear. A fifth, Eugene Dennis, the party's general secretary, had intended to go into hiding but ended up turning himself in when the arrangements got messed up. Of the four who did not appear, Gus Hall was arrested a few weeks later in Mexico. Robert Thompson was taken into custody a year afterward in a cabin in the Sierras. Two others, Gil Green and Henry Winston, stayed in hiding for five years and eventually turned themselves in voluntarily to serve their sentences.

The course followed by the CP leadership was costly. It made no political sense to follow such a split policy. Many members concluded that the outcome reflected paralysis, even panic, in the party leadership. Many CP activists read the decision as a signal that pulling back from public political activity was necessary. A substantial number of secondary leaders dropped out of public view, even though they were not facing any charges. Many cadres severed connections to the party. Some who still considered themselves communists went to the extremes of burning their Marxist books or sealing them in crates and burying them in backyards or hiding them in basements.

An indication of the CP leadership's panicky retreat was its response to the arrest and trial of the Rosenbergs and Sobell, who were charged with having been Communist Party members who spied for the Soviet Union. The case against them was cooked up by the FBI and the Justice Department. The prosecution included secret—and illegal—collaboration between the judge and government lawyers. The frame-up artists in the Justice Department drew on deep prejudices, including anti-Semitism, to make their slanders stick.[10]

Although the Rosenbergs were known to many of their comrades as having been members of the CP, the party leadership decided not to acknowledge this fact publicly. It was not until the mid-1970s, after the Rosenbergs' two sons published a book proudly defending their parents' Communist Party affiliation,[11] that many CP members would publicly acknowledge that the two victims of McCarthyite reaction had been party members.

Julius and Ethel Rosenberg were arrested in the summer of 1950 and tried and convicted in March 1951. Throughout this time, no defense committee was organized to expose the frame-up and mobilize opposition to the charges. Neither the Communist Party nor the defendants took any initiative in this direction. The CP leadership apparently hoped in this way to insulate the party against government accusations that some in its ranks had engaged in espionage for the Soviet Union. This dissociation from the defendants was carried so far that the *Daily Worker* did not even report on the trial, publishing only a short three-sentence news item on a back page when the guilty verdict was returned.

It was only after the death sentence was pronounced on April 5, 1951, that the *Daily Worker* condemned the frame-up and barbaric penalty. But even then, no defense committee was initiated. Finally, several months later, the *National Guardian* (now the *Guardian*), a New York radical weekly, launched a campaign to expose the frame-up and to seek to block the executions. This led in November 1951 to the formation of the National Committee to Secure

Justice in the Rosenberg Case. Many CP members joined in activities organized by the committee, as did many other individuals and some organizations, including the Socialist Workers Party.

The McCarthy era is sometimes referred to as a period during which the CP functioned in a partially underground way. But this is not true in any meaningful sense. The CP had no underground party press and no political activity of any kind organized in clandestinity. When CP leaders went "underground," they removed themselves from public political activity—though rarely from FBI surveillance. The "underground" organizers stayed in touch with party structures, such as they were, participated in leadership discussions through articles in the party's discussion bulletins and attendance at committee meetings, and waited for the political situation to change.

In fact, any real underground functioning would have been ludicrous, since the CP was never legally proscribed throughout this entire period, despite government attempts in that direction. The repression hit hard at CP members and former members. A total of 160 people in the United States and Puerto Rico were arrested on charges under the Smith Act; forty-one eventually served prison terms. Many individuals, CP members and others, were victimized through blacklisting, FBI harassment, blackmail, and deportation or threat of deportation. Others were imprisoned for refusing to inform on their comrades when called before witch-hunting bodies such as the House Un-American Activities Committee.

But the government's attempts to outlaw the CP failed. Repeated efforts to force it to register members' names with the Justice Department were stymied in the courts and finally defeated. The party's publications, including the *Daily Worker*, continued to be printed legally and sent through the mails without restriction.

Most members of the Communist Party did not identify themselves as communists, even to their fellow workers and others they collaborated with in political activity. But this policy did not begin with the witch hunt; it began and became generalized during the Popular Front period. Far from an aid to the Communist Party in combating attacks on the democratic rights of its members and supporters, this policy made CP members especially vulnerable to the witch-hunters. Congressional committees and right-wingers specialized in "naming names" of Communist Party members and those accused of being members. Members of the CP who had concealed their affiliation from co-workers and those with whom they collaborated in political activity faced self-imposed obstacles in organizing support for their democratic rights as members of the CP. Those who were more widely known as CP members were less easily victimized by the McCarthyite "investigators."

Much of the ground lost for public functioning by the CP was not terrain given up inch by inch in determined battle for democratic rights, but was forfeited as a result of the party's political crisis. In the labor movement, large numbers of workers were ready to extend a generous helping hand of working-class solidarity to all victims of right-wing reaction and government repression. Others, especially in the Black community, recognized the need for united action to defend the rights of minority viewpoints and democratic rights in general. But the Stalinist leaders, exaggerating the fascist threat, kept their backs turned to the ranks of labor and its allies. Their course increased the damage inflicted by the witch hunt on the Communist Party and on the working-class movement as a whole.

FBI's covert operations

With the end of the Korean War in 1953 and the repudiation of Senator Joseph McCarthy by the dominant sections of the ruling class the following year, the witch hunt began to wane. The political situation in the country shifted. In 1954, the Black-led fight for civil rights, which had continued without letup since World War II, won an historic victory when the US Supreme Court ruled that school segregation violated the Constitution. This in turn spurred further fights against Jim Crow segregation. Public opposition to further prosecutions under the Smith Act also grew. Those who fought back against violations of constitutional rights—encouraged by groups such as the newly formed Emergency Civil Liberties Committee (ECLC)—were able to score victories, including some favorable rulings in the federal courts.

In 1956 the National Security Council convened a special meeting in the White House to hear a report and consider proposals from FBI Director Hoover on how to counter the stiffening popular resistance to government moves against the Bill of Rights. The facts about this meeting were first revealed in 1981 during the trial of the SWP lawsuit, when Justice Department officials introduced into evidence a report on the meeting previously classified top secret. The document was submitted in an effort—ultimately unsuccessful—to show that the FBI's covert "Counter-Intelligence Program" (Cointelpro) was lawful on the grounds that it had been set in motion at this NSC meeting, where it received presidential approval.

To explain the document's significance, the government lawyers called to the witness stand Herbert Brownell, who had served as attorney general in President Dwight Eisenhower's cabinet. Brownell testified that those present at the 1956 NSC meeting included Eisenhower, Vice-president Richard Nixon, CIA chief Allen Dulles, FBI director Hoover, and other government officials. At the meeting, Hoover outlined the situation. The government's efforts to disrupt the operations of the Communist Party, the Socialist Workers Party, and other groups were running into greater public opposition, he said. This was being reflected in the growing reluctance by federal judges to sustain prosecutions under the Smith Act, to uphold denials of passports to "subversives," and to approve other witch-hunting measures such as driving communists out of the merchant marine by lifting their seaman's papers.

"To illustrate," Hoover told the National Security Council, "42 prominent persons, including Mrs. Franklin D. Roosevelt, Norman Thomas, Henry Steele Commager, and many others who should know better, recently signed a petition calling for amnesty for persons now serving prison terms for Smith Act convictions and a cessation of further prosecution." Hoover went on to complain bitterly about court rulings "such as the Judge Youngdahl decision in the passport case of Leonard Boudin on November 22, 1953, and the actions of the Circuit Court of Appeals for the Ninth circuit, San Francisco, California, ruling out the Coast Guard screening program [for the merchant marine] on October 26, 1955...."

Fortunately, Hoover emphasized, the power of the government's executive branch to act was not restricted to what the people of the country would support and the federal courts would accept. What could not be accomplished openly could be achieved covertly. The FBI possessed the weapon of "counterintelligence." Hoover proudly reported, "We have sought to infiltrate, penetrate, disorganize, and disrupt the [Communist] party.... Informants have been the key to penetration of the party.... We currently have 921 active informants operating in the security field, providing hourly intelligence reflecting the innermost plans and policies of the Communist Party."

On the witness stand in 1981, Brownell stressed that Hoover's report covered not just the Communist Party itself, but also "those who were aiding it in various ways. For example there were some splinter groups which sent representatives to international communist meetings, secret meetings, things of that sort. They were included in what we call the subversive groups who were operating secretly in conjunction with foreign powers." This included the Socialist Workers Party, the former attorney general added.

Brownell was asked to identify "the source of the authority for the FBI to conduct the countermeasures as set forth in this page against the Communist Party and other subversive groups." "Presidential directive," he shot back. "I think the legal situation was that the President did not give any restriction to the methods that were to be used to accomplish the ends that he sought." The techniques approved by the National Security Council included disruption operations by informers, break-ins, wiretaps, and microphone bugs installed without warrants, as well as opening the mail and sorting through discarded trash of "subversive" targets. Six months later, the FBI formally inaugurated its Cointelpro operations, first against the CP, then against the SWP, Black organizations fighting for civil rights, and others.

If the majority of US people could no longer be mobilized to support the openly proclaimed goal of breaking up communist groups by government prosecution and blacklisting, the National Security Council had decided, then the FBI would wage a secret operation against the "subversives".

The expansion of the FBI's covert operations against critics of government policy took place at a time when the right to organize political activity was being extended. This advance was a by-product of the revival of working-class political action represented by the growth of the civil rights struggle, particularly in the segregated South. Despite continuation of the trade union movement's political retreat, the new rise in the struggle waged by Black people was registering important conquests. In the course of the battle to bring the Jim Crow structures crashing down, the civil rights movement was expanding the room for individuals and groups to organize to fight for their interests without government interference.

The most far-reaching conquest in this area was extension of the First Amendment guarantee of freedom of association to include the right of organizations to privacy from government cops and regulation. This victory was codified in a string of civil rights cases. One of the first and most important of these was won by the NAACP against the Alabama state government. This battle grew out of the NAACP's support for the Montgomery, Alabama, bus boycott, which began in December 1955 and ended with the desegregation of that city's buses. In retaliation for activities such as this, Alabama officials tried to force the NAACP to register the names and addresses of its members and contributors with the state. The NAACP refused, arguing that its list of members and supporters was no business of the government, and that if the names were turned over this would result in victimization of individuals.

In 1958, the US Supreme Court ruled in favor of the NAACP, affirming that there is a "vital relationship between freedom to associate and privacy in one's associations." The court held that "Inviolability of privacy in group associations may in many circumstances be indispensable to preservation of freedom of association, particularly where a group espouses dissident beliefs." (This constitutional right to privacy was extended still further in 1973, when the Supreme Court ruled that a "right of personal privacy . . . does exist under the Constitution" and that it "is broad enough to encompass a woman's decision on whether or not to terminate her pregnancy.")

From the standpoint of the executive branch of the government, however, these court rulings did not affect covert FBI operations in the United States. These operations, the Justice Department maintained, derived their justification from the "inherent powers of the president," and were beyond the reach of court rulings and laws passed by Congress. So long as these operations remained hidden, or largely hidden, from public view, this position was not put to the test. But when the covert operations began to be exposed in the early 1970s, the issue was joined. The result has been the posing of the most fundamental questions of constitutional rights, many of which have been presented directly as a result of the SWP's legal initiative against the attorney general and the FBI.

Forcing government operations to light

The SWP lawsuit was filed in July 1973 as the Watergate scandal was breaking. Watergate was the first governmental crisis resulting from the growing contradiction in the latter part of the twentieth century between what the US ruling class is compelled to do against its class enemies at home and abroad, and what it can openly proclaim as its goals and methods.

In the Second World War, the country's rulers were able to mobilize the country behind their war aims. Those who opposed this course were in a small minority; some were imprisoned for their minority views without a major national outcry. By the time of the Korean War, however, there was little enthusiasm among working people for the war, and a good deal of opposition was openly expressed. A measure of this shift was the decision by the government not to seek a declaration of war by Congress as required under the Constitution. The Korean War was also the first war the United States failed to win.

When the US government escalated its intervention in Vietnam in the mid-1960s, conditions existed, for the first time in the history of the country, for the emergence of a massive antiwar movement in the middle of a shooting war. Antiwar sentiment was accompanied by deepening popular suspicion and distrust of the secrecy and lies of Washington about its war aims and its methods. As in the Korean War, there was no declaration of war proposed to Congress. The government acted throughout on the basis of "executive power."

As the Watergate revelations developed, it became clear to a growing number of people that the lies and covert operations that were used by the government to further its aims in Vietnam were the very methods it used at home. The "inherent powers" that the president used to wage a murderous war against the peoples of Indochina were also being used against fighters for Black rights, against Puerto Rican and Mexican-American activists, against the women's liberation movement, against antiwar organizations, and against communists. As more of the truth about Cointelpro and other covert FBI operations began to emerge, it further became clear that these methods had been used *at home first*. Washington's wars against its class enemies overseas are an extension of the capitalist government's war against its domestic class enemies.

Today the US government is in the midst of a second crisis, triggered by the exposure of the secret Iran arms deal and the covert funding of the *contras* trying to overthrow the government of Nicaragua. Like Watergate, the current crisis has its roots in the inability of US imperialism to stop the march of history. The US rulers must increasingly turn to covert operations to carry out policies and employ methods that they cannot openly proclaim or defend, and at least some of these covert operations are inevitably exposed publicly.

The SWP suit against the government has attracted new attention and broader support as the current government crisis has developed, since the issues at the heart of the case are the very questions posed by the contragate scandal: Can the rule of law be suspended in the name of "national security"? Are the president, the attorney general, the CIA, the FBI, and the National Security Council above the law?

The depth of what is at stake was revealed in a dramatic confrontation that occurred during the pretrial battles in the SWP case. From the outset, the most important issue in the case was whether or not the FBI has a legal right to use covert informers to spy on and disrupt the SWP and YSA. To help prove that this government practice violated constitutional rights, the SWP's lawyers asked that Judge Griesa order the FBI to turn over the files on its informers. The judge ordered that a sample consisting of files on eighteen informers be produced. The Justice Department immediately appealed that order, first to the Court of Appeals and then to the United States Supreme Court. Turning over *any* informer files, government lawyers argued, would breach the absolute rule that the identity of undercover informers can never be disclosed without their agreement. To allow this principle to be violated would have "a devastating impact on the overall investigative effectiveness of the FBI," Justice Department lawyers contended. The higher courts nonetheless declined to reverse Griesa's order.

The government then took an unprecedented step: Attorney General Griffin Bell (a member of President James Carter's cabinet) informed Judge Griesa that he was refusing to obey the order. It was one of the moments in the case when the routine legal maneuvering between lawyers was suspended. The attorney general was acting not as a political appointee but as the direct spokesperson for the police power of the government, of the state power itself. Griesa responded by finding the attorney general in contempt of court, on June 30, 1978, the first such ruling in US history. "The Attorney General has no 'right' to defy a court order," declared Griesa. "The Court possesses and must possess under our system of law, the authority to enforce an order for the production of evidence. . . ."

The Justice Department immediately appealed the contempt ruling. The Court of Appeals, which had earlier refused to overturn Griesa's order, now ruled that a contempt finding was too drastic a sanction for Bell's defiance of a court order and reversed the ruling. The contents of the files were eventually summarized by a special appointee of the court and this summary was made part of the trial record.

In a television interview show in 1977, former President Richard Nixon was asked whether he believed that a president could authorize illegal acts such as burglaries against opponents of the Vietnam War. He answered:

When the President does it, that means that it is not illegal.

QUESTION: By definition?
ANSWER: Exactly. Exactly. If the President, for example, approves something because of the national security . . . then the President's decision in that instance is one that enables those who carry it out, to carry it out without violating a law.

The same position was argued at great length by Justice Department officials in the trial of the SWP lawsuit. The former attorney general, Herbert Brownell, testified about a document he had written in 1954 in response to a Supreme Court decision that the cops had violated the Fourth Amendment by breaking into a private home and planting a microphone in the bedroom of a man accused of gambling violations. Brownell directed the FBI to ignore the ruling when going after "subversives." Brownell wrote:

> Obviously the installation of a microphone in a bedroom or some comparably intimate location should be avoided wherever possible. It may appear, however, that important intelligence or evidence relating to matters connected with the national security can only be obtained by the installation of a microphone in such a location. It is my opinion that under such circumstances the installation is proper and is not prohibited by the Supreme Court decision. . . .

On the witness stand, Brownell argued that when it came to "intelligence" or "national security" investigations—that is, when the target is political, rather than criminal, activity—the executive branch of government has the authority to ignore the Bill of Rights. Under cross-examination the former attorney general became visibly irritated that anyone could question this doctrine. When the judge himself asked some pointed questions, Brownell's voice hardened. Finally, he was asked whether it was "your view as the Attorney General that the Fourth Amendment was applicable to intelligence investigations?" Brownell responded:

> We didn't have any guidance from the Supreme Court on that. I think the matter is still open as far as the Supreme Court is concerned. On the one hand you have the express

powers of the president to conduct foreign affairs and to be the Commander in Chief. On the other hand you have the Fourth Amendment.

Brownell then paused, glared directly at Griesa, and said, "So far there has been no court decision which prohibited such activities in the field of intelligence."

The message was unambiguous: this has been going on for a long time and no federal judge has ever tried to stop us, so don't make trouble for yourself. Griesa reserved response until his ruling, which explicitly rejected the claim by Brownell and the Justice Department that the executive branch has the power to trample on the Bill of Rights.

Why the Socialist Workers Party?

Why was it the SWP that was able to take the initiative in this fight for democratic rights? Why didn't the Communist Party, which has been hit harder than the SWP by government harassment, spying, and disruption, take such a step once the opportunity presented itself? Why wasn't such a move made by a social democratic organization such as the Democratic Socialists of America, which could call on legal and financial resources far greater than those available to the SWP suit?

The answers to these questions shed important light on the results of the differing perspectives of the major currents in the working-class movement today. A look at some of the ways the Justice Department attempted to derail and defeat the SWP case helps to clarify the fundamental questions involved.

One of the government's tactics was repeated attempts from 1976 through 1980 to persuade the SWP to settle the case out of court. The proposed terms of the settlement were as follows: the FBI would pledge to obey the law, but make no specific mention of barring such methods as informers, burglaries, and disruption operations. In return for the SWP's acceptance of this promise and dropping its suit, the Justice Department would agree to a substantial financial payment to the party.

The government did reach such settlements in a number of other lawsuits against the FBI. Many of these cases had been inspired by the early successes of the SWP suit in forcing into the open previously secret FBI operations. Some of these cases were settled when the individuals or groups who brought them were unable to sustain the burden of an expensive and time-consuming court fight against the vast resources of the federal government. Other lawsuits, however, were settled because the plaintiffs were politically persuaded that FBI "guidelines" announced by the Justice Department in 1976 essentially accomplished what they had set out to achieve and there was no reason to press further.[12] Those who agreed to settlements on this basis refused to challenge the US government's claim that it must have a political police force to defend "us" against "them"—whether "they" are subversives, terrorists, or the world communist movement. Those whose goal was to try to get the FBI and other federal police agencies to operate in a more enlightened and democratic way were paralyzed when it came to forcing the real questions of democratic liberties into the forefront.

The SWP took a different course. As the SWP case headed toward trial, the Justice Department stepped up efforts to achieve an out-of-court settlement. Sporadic probes by government lawyers had been made for several years, as other cases were settled. Boudin and the SWP did not rule out a possible settlement and explored every proposal. But each turned out to offer no concrete conquests for democratic rights. In the spring and summer of 1980, Justice Department lawyers renewed their efforts, significantly raising the amount of money offered. (It was estimated that the final payment could go as high as a million dollars, including payments for attorneys' fees.) But there was no substantive change in the content of the agreement proposed by Washington.

In September 1980 the Attorney General's office submitted a "final" offer for settlement. It followed the basic pattern of other settlements reached in suits brought by victims of FBI operations. In response, Leonard Boudin sent a detailed letter to the Justice Department spelling out the reasons for rejecting the proposal. He wrote:

> It is inconceivable to me that *SWP v. Attorney General* could or should be settled without addressing the violations of the Bill of Rights by the defendants, and affirming the rights of the plaintiffs to be free of government harassment, victimization, blacklisting, and "investigation," whether of the Cointelpro type, or the more routine varieties. It is my view that Judge Griesa, who has spent seven years supervising discovery in this action, will not approve any settlement of this case that fails to face these issues squarely.
>
> The Attorney General's office has been evading the constitutional issues posed by FBI, CIA, and other defendant agencies' wrongdoing ever since the major public revelations of the mid-1970s focused public opinion on these "intelligence" agencies. Congress, despite many hearings and much discussion of a charter for the FBI, has not come to grips with these questions. Settlements like the one reached in [Jane] *Fonda* [*v. the FBI* and] *Alliance to End Repression v. Chicago*, likewise skirt the issues that, from the standpoint of constitutional rights, are paramount. . . .

The extraordinary record that has been developed in this case over seven years establishes that plaintiffs have engaged solely in activities that are protected by the First Amendment. Plaintiffs have a right to pursue these activities free from investigation, disruption, and penalization of any kind by the government. The entire purpose of this litigation is to vindicate that First Amendment right.

One provision of the Justice Department's "final" offer was especially troubling to Boudin and the SWP. The government draft settlement stated that the SWP's "activities and advocacy of ideas shown in the record in this case do not constitute a sufficient basis for initiating a domestic security investigation of plaintiffs under current law and guidelines. . . ." But elsewhere the document stated that the court record "does not consist of all the information available to the FBI."

The maneuver was transparent. The government wanted to be able to continue to claim that there was evidence of crimes by the SWP that had not been submitted to the court in order to protect supersecret sources and methods of obtaining information. "If there is any such evidence," Boudin responded, "it should be produced. If there isn't, it should be stated that none exists."

This issue emerged as a central one at the trial, which opened in April 1981. Early in the proceedings, the government lawyers announced that the FBI had compiled evidence of illegal activities by the SWP. This evidence, they said, provided legal justification for all the FBI's actions against the SWP. The sources and methods by which this information was obtained were so sensitive, however, that revealing the evidence to the SWP would bring grave consequences for "national security."

The government's strategy was more dangerous than

might appear at first glance. Under court rules of evidence, material withheld from one side cannot be considered because there is no opportunity to rebut the evidence or question witnesses about it. Judges normally refuse to consider such "secret evidence." And that was Griesa's initial ruling: if the Justice Department did not want to disclose the contents of the secret material, then he would not consider it in reaching his decision in the case.

But this course posed a danger. Even if Griesa refused to consider the secret material as evidence, the material could nonetheless become part of the record in the case in an appeal to a higher court. Thus, an appeals court could not only read the secret material but even base a ruling on it. Although extremely rare, it was not unheard-of for courts to consider such secret materials.

For this reason, the SWP took an unusual—in fact unprecedented—step. The party asked Griesa to consider and weigh the secret material. Although the party's lawyers would not be able to rebut the documents directly since they would remain in the dark about the allegations contained in them, the judge could evaluate the charges in light of the totality of facts that would be presented in the trial. On that basis, the judge could decide for himself whether the accusations in the secret material were credible.

This move surprised the judge and caught the government lawyers off guard. Griesa listened carefully as attorney Margaret Winter, who headed the SWP legal team at the trial, argued that only if the judge examined the secret files could the party hope to remove what could become a major, even fatal, obstacle to a ruling favorable to the SWP in the Court of Appeals or Supreme Court. Griesa understood and agreed with the point. There followed a series of private meetings between the judge and government attorneys, in which Griesa evidently put considerable pressure on the Justice Department either to voluntarily withdraw the secret material or disclose its contents so the SWP could read it.

Finally, Griesa announced a ruling on the issue that, he stated, represented "in part, an agreement by the Government." The judge would give "no evidentiary consideration whatever" to the secret materials and the Justice Department "has agreed that it will not rely on these matters as evidence in this court or in any Appellate Court." The government lawyers had been forced to agree to forego relying on the secret file in any appeal in the lawsuit.

The episode highlighted a fundamental fact about the Socialist Workers Party. To this day, one can only guess at the contents of the secret file. Yet the SWP had no hesitation in urging the judge to read and consider it. A similar question had arisen earlier in the case when the Justice Department was objecting to turning over secret FBI informer files. Leonard Boudin then recommended to the SWP leadership that it agree to let Griesa read the files himself since Griesa was not yet prepared to overrule the FBI claims of "informer privilege."

Looking back on that decision later, Boudin viewed it as a turning point in the case. "I will never forget when Judge Griesa walked into the courtroom after reviewing those FBI informer reports," he said. "Of course he was barred from revealing anything about the content of the files. But he turned to me and said, 'Mr. Boudin, you would never believe what is in those files.' He was shocked by the kind of information on legal political activity and details of personal lives that the FBI was compiling."

It was not a difficult decision for the Socialist Workers Party to agree to the judge reading the informer files and then the secret file, even though the party was denied the right to see the materials itself. The SWP was confident that nothing in the secret files would show policies or actions of the party that would contradict what the SWP said publicly. (Of course, no one could be sure that the FBI did not concoct such evidence—indeed it was assumed they had. But any such manufactured material would be contradicted by the massive factual record based on decades of activity in the working-class movement.) This confidence was based on a fundamental political fact. The Socialist Workers Party, like all genuinely communist organizations, *has no special goals of its own as a party.* It analyzes the stage of development of the worldwide struggle of the working class and its allies. The party offers proposals for how best to advance along the lines indicated by that struggle that will lead to the conquest of power by the workers and farmers. Because the SWP has no special goals of its own, separate from the historic course along which the working class is marching, it can have no program or policies kept secret from the working class. Moreover, any organizational practices or structures not consistent with this would cut across the party's political perspectives.

This principle was established with the founding of the modern communist movement 140 years ago. Marx and Engels fought in 1847 to free the newly formed Communist League from the conspiratorial traditions and organizational methods that had up until then dominated the league's forerunners and the revolutionary workers' movement in general. Secret structures, a secret program, even a secret language—all had to give way to a movement that consciously rejected conspiracy as a mode of functioning, Marx and Engels insisted.

As the opening lines of the *Communist Manifesto* itself put it, "It is high time that Communists should openly, in the face of the whole world, publish their views, their aims, their tendencies and meet this nursery tale of the Spectre of Communism with a Manifesto of the party itself."

This approach flowed from the rejection of any idea that a real revolution can be carried out by a small group acting on behalf of the working class. A "true revolution is the exact opposite of the ideas of a *mouchard* [police informer], who . . . sees in every revolution the work of a small coterie," Marx explained.

At the SWP trial, the *mouchards* kept trying to prove that the party said one thing in public and something different in its closed meetings. They tried to establish that the party maintained dual structures, one for public purposes and the other hidden from view. In every case, the facts showed the opposite. While a workers' party has the right, in fact the responsibility, to protect the privacy of its members and supporters from the bosses and the police, it has no right to keep its ideas, methods, and organizational concepts hidden from working people. If the SWP had, at any time in its history, adopted any other course or engaged in specific activities that contradicted this policy, the SWP lawsuit against the FBI would have been precluded. The party would have been paralyzed by concern that a trial might well expose a duplicitous history.

As the trial demonstrated, the FBI's accusations of conspiracy and hidden goals were *pure projection*. It turned out to be the White House and FBI, not the SWP, that conceal their true aims and methods. It turned out to be the White House and FBI, not the SWP, that maintain a covert structure to carry out what they cannot openly proclaim. It turned out to be the White House and FBI, not the SWP, that rely on conspiratorial modes of operation to achieve their goals behind the backs of the people of the United States.

Social democratic forces in the United States were incapable of taking an initiative like that of the SWP in defense of democratic rights because their starting point is to convince the exploited that they share common interests with "democratic" elements among the US rulers. Their framework is to bring these more enlightened forces into positions of power and administration of the capitalist state, including its political police apparatus. These socialists do not rule out the day when they will share administrative duties in a capitalist government, including in running the police—as their counterparts have done in many countries in the world. In this position, they would be loyal defenders of the capitalist state.

The Communist Party, for equally important political reasons, could not take an initiative like the one taken by the SWP. The CP long ago departed from the communist starting point of seeking to advance the struggle of the working class of the United States, as part of the world working class, along its historically necessary line of march. This had been replaced by the starting point of the diplomatic interests of the Soviet regime. Once the Stalinists set out along this road, they abandoned the principle of telling the truth to the working class about their political aims and organizational forms. As a result, they became vulnerable to government frame-ups and witch-hunting smear campaigns, which they were handicapped in combating.

The consequences of this course blocked the CP from leading the fight to expose capitalist frame-ups such as the one against the Rosenbergs and made it impossible for the CP to take a political and legal offensive against the FBI such as the campaign set in motion by the SWP, which has had such positive results for the democratic rights of the people of the United States.

Expansion of political rights

Judge Griesa handed down his opinion in the SWP case in August 1986. The ruling is a victory for political rights, codifying in a court opinion for the first time many rights and liberties that have been fought for over many years. By vindicating these rights, the decision further strengthens them, giving an important new weapon that can be used by others in future battles for prosecution against secret police spying, disruption, and harassment.

Griesa's 210-page ruling affirms the constitutional freedoms claimed by the SWP and YSA. The court found that the FBI disruption program, the "black bag job" break-ins at SWP and YSA offices, and the use of undercover informers constituted "violations of the constitutional rights of the SWP and lacked legislative or regulatory authority."

Leonard Boudin said of the consequences of this ruling: "The impact of this decision goes far beyond the SWP and YSA. It is a contribution to constitutional law, extending important new protections to the rights of all politically active individuals and organizations." The ruling expands the space for political activity and individual privacy for everyone in this country. It strengthens constitutional protection against government meddling in people's private affairs and in the affairs of groups to which they belong.

The court ruling includes the following points:

- The constitutional right of privacy includes protection against the use of government informers to infiltrate a political organization. The decision is unambiguous: "The FBI's use of informants clearly constituted invasion of privacy." Drawing on past precedents such as the victory of the NAACP against the state of Alabama, the court reaffirmed that in addition to the rights of individuals "an association has a right of privacy" under the Constitution.

- FBI break-ins in the name of "national security" were violations of the SWP's rights under the Fourth Amendment to the Constitution, which bars arbitrary searches by government agents. These burglaries, Griesa wrote, "were invasions of privacy of the most aggravated form. The FBI's own nomenclature—'bag jobs' and 'black bag jobs'—indicates something of the nature of these stealthy invasions of private premises for the purpose of obtaining private information."

- The FBI's Cointelpro operations "were patently unconstitutional and violated the SWP's First Amendment rights of free speech and assembly. Moreover, there was no statutory or regulatory authority for the FBI to disrupt the SWP's lawful political activities."

- Victims of such FBI operations are entitled to collect money damages from the government in compensation. Griesa awarded the SWP and YSA $125,000 for invasion of privacy by informers, $96,500 for invasion of privacy by FBI burglaries, and $42,500 for specific Cointelpro operations.

In reaching these specific conclusions, Griesa dealt with

even more far-reaching questions of constitutional law. He rejected the claim that what top White House officials often called the presidents' "inherent power" allowed them to ignore constitutional rights in the name of "national security." The Justice Department had argued that the SWP could not claim damages for the FBI operations because of a provision in federal law making the government immune to lawsuits for actions that fall within the government's "discretion," even when "the discretion involved is abused." But the government "cannot have discretion to behave unconstitutionally," Griesa ruled.

These findings were strengthened further by the judge's decision that the SWP is entitled to an injunction that will prevent the FBI or any other government agency from using files containing information that was obtained illegally by the FBI. (As of this writing, the judge has not issued an order spelling out the details of this injunction.)[13] This illegally obtained information is being used to victimize people who are or have been members of the YSA or the SWP in the past or who have expressed support for or interest in these organizations. The dossiers are used to discriminate against noncitizens who apply for citizenship papers, permanent residence, or visas to visit the country. They are used to justify denials of security clearances for workers in factories with military contracts, leading to harassment, denials of promotions, or even firings. They are used to single out government workers for special interrogation or as the basis for denying jobs at the post office or in other federal agencies.

How many files are there? The FBI alone admits to maintaining *ten million pages* on the SWP and YSA and individuals associated with these organizations.

Once Judge Griesa decides on the extent of the injunction on the files, his ruling on the case as a whole will be entered, and the stage of appeals will begin. During the legal arguments regarding the terms of the proposed injunction, the Justice Department gave a preview of the arguments it will use to try to get Griesa's entire opinion overturned. In court papers, Justice Department officials argued that barring the use of the files on the SWP and YSA will place at risk "the Nation's vital interests of self-preservation." Attorney General Edwin Meese's lawyers invoked the decision of the US Supreme Court in 1951 upholding the Smith Act convictions of the Communist Party leaders: "The Supreme Court has noted that self-preservation is the 'ultimate value of any society.'" The need to protect this "ultimate value" overrides constitutional protections of the rights of groups and individuals, they argue. Moreover, the Justice Department insists, the fact that the FBI could come up with no evidence of SWP lawbreaking after decades of investigation did not of itself make the investigation or the techniques used in it illegal—"the FBI was *and is* authorized to conduct such investigations." (Emphasis added.)

In the nearly five decades since the US government unleashed the FBI in a war against political rights and democratic liberties, the vanguard of the working-class movement has learned invaluable lessons about the importance of the fight for democratic rights. The consequences of not defending the rights of those one may have political disagreements with have been painfully evident. The negative results of policies that require sacrificing the fight for democratic rights in the name of some seemingly more important objective have been seen. The importance of the conquests won by the Black movement and labor for the right to organize and for privacy of association has become better appreciated by politically conscious workers and farmers in the United States.

In the course of its lawsuit against the government, the SWP itself has acquired a far richer and more complete understanding of its own fight for the codification in a court ruling of its rights and the rights of its members and supporters—a ruling that also will be used by others. The decision that has been won is a genuine acquisition for the democratic rights of the people of the United States. Defending that conquest against efforts to weaken it or overturn it in the higher courts is a battle that should be joined by everyone—in the United States and around the world—who understands that a blow to the US secret police and a victory for democratic rights in the United States will be a gain for working people everywhere.

Imperialist war and the working class

Farrell Dobbs

In 1949 Farrell Dobbs wrote the following introduction to the third edition of *Socialism on Trial* by James P. Cannon. That book presents Cannon's testimony from the 1941 federal court trial of leaders of the Socialist Workers Party and of Local 544-CIO described earlier in these pages in the section "Frame-up in Minneapolis."

Both Cannon and Dobbs were among the eighteen defendants who were convicted and imprisoned, in their cases at Sandstone federal penitentiary in Minnesota. They, along with ten other defendants, were sentenced to sixteen months and served almost thirteen, from December 31, 1943, to January 24, 1945. Six other defendants were given one-year terms and served ten months.

The frame-up of the eighteen was the first use of the Smith "Gag" Act, signed into law by President Franklin Roosevelt in June 1940. This reactionary legislation was aimed at silencing the class-struggle vanguard of the unions and broader working-class movement that was organizing and leading opposition to

Washington's preparations to drag workers and farmers in the United States into the imperialist slaughter of World War II.

Cannon was a founding leader of the communist movement in the United States in 1919 and national secretary of the Socialist Workers Party.

Dobbs was a central leader of the Teamster strikes in Minneapolis in 1934 and of the campaign to organize over-the-road truckers in much of the Midwest from 1937 to early 1940. Those battles transformed the Teamsters union in that region into a fighting proletarian social movement, helped pave the way for the organization of industrial unions nationwide, and pointed the road toward independent working-class political action.

From 1940 Dobbs shouldered responsibilities in the SWP's central leadership. These included national labor secretary, national organization secretary, editor of the *Militant*, and, from 1953 to 1972, the party's national secretary. Dobbs was the SWP's candidate for president of the United States four times between 1948 and 1960.

As he was preparing this introduction to *Socialism on Trial* in early 1949, Dobbs was also writing weekly coverage for the *Militant* newspaper of a second major Smith Act trial—the prosecution in federal court in New York City's Foley Square of eleven leaders of the Communist Party. All were convicted and ten given the maximum sentence of five years.

Dobbs's introduction sheds political light on central questions addressed in "Fifty Years of Covert Operations in the US: Washington's Political Police and the American Working Class."

∾

Socialism On Trial is the verbatim testimony of James P. Cannon, national secretary of the Socialist Workers Party, in the 1941 Minneapolis trial of eighteen Trotskyists under the thought-control Smith Act. The salient facts about the trial and conviction are related in Joseph Hansen's introduction to the second edition, which is reprinted in this volume.[1]

Dealing with the whole range of Marxism, Comrade Cannon's testimony in that famous trial has become recognized as the simplest and best introduction to an understanding of the major questions of revolutionary socialist program and tactics. It is the most popular pamphlet ever published by our movement. Two large editions of *Socialism On Trial* have already been exhausted.

The republication of this testimony in the Minneapolis trial is given added timeliness by the coincidence that, as this third edition goes to press, eleven leaders of the Stalinist Communist Party are on trial in a federal court in New York City. This new prosecution is a striking confirmation of Comrade Cannon's prediction, in the Minneapolis court, that the assault on civil liberties which began with the prosecution of the Trotskyists would be later directed against other organizations.

The Stalinists supported the government in its prosecution of the eighteen Trotskyists and applauded their conviction and imprisonment. But this treacherous conduct did not save them when their own time came. It did not even save them from the truly ironical circumstance that the indictment brought against them alleges violation of the Smith Act—the very same law under which the Trotskyists were tried and convicted in Minneapolis.[2]

The real aim of the capitalist government in these thought-control prosecutions is to outlaw Marxism. It is therefore extremely important to know exactly what true Marxism is. But that knowledge cannot be gained from the Stalinists who have twisted, distorted, perverted, and betrayed the Marxist program in so many ways. Marxism has a right to be defended by its genuine exponents.

Under these circumstances, publication of this edition

of *Socialism On Trial* serves an especially vital need. In it will be found a true explanation of Marxism, set forth in clear and simple terms.

I wish to call attention particularly to the remarks about war and democracy. In these pages will be found Comrade Cannon's answers on these vital questions during direct examination by defense counsel. He explains that imperialist wars to capture new markets, sources of raw materials, and fields of investment are inevitable so long as capitalism continues in existence. The Socialist Workers Party is unalterably opposed to any and all imperialist wars.

"It is absolutely true that Hitler wants to dominate the world," Comrade Cannon said, "but we think it is equally true that the ruling group of American capitalists has the same idea, and we are not in favor of either of them.

"We do not think that the Sixty Families who own America want to wage this war for some sacred principle of democracy. We think they are the greatest enemies of democracy here at home. We think they would only use the opportunity of a war to eliminate all civil liberties at home, to get the best imitation of fascism they can possibly get."[3]

These significant words were spoken seven years ago, on the eve of the formal entry of the United States government into the Second World War. (The eighteen defendants in the Minneapolis Trial were sentenced to prison on December 8, 1941, at the same hour war was being declared by Congress.) These words gave an accurate forecast of the present campaign to crush civil rights in this country in preparation for a new war to conquer the world.

The special prosecutor, who was later rewarded with a federal judgeship, sought on cross-examination to refute these predictions. The resulting clash brought a more precise spelling out of the war aims of American imperialism and the terrible consequences to the working people. Listen to these quotations, for example.

"Once they have deprived the workers of the right to strike on so-called patriotic pretexts," Comrade Cannon predicted, "then the capitalists will begin squeezing down wages and refusing concessions." Truer words were never spoken, as every worker knows today after the wartime wage freeze in the face of a steeply rising cost of living.

"The next thing that will probably appear on the horizon," he continued, "is attempts of these Sixty Families and their supporters to stop the popularizing of ideas inimical to the capitalists, and to check by legislation the organization of the workers."[4]

When that prediction was made back in 1941, the capitalists were grinding out propaganda about a holy war to defend the "four freedoms." Comrade Cannon's warning was like a cry in the wilderness. Yet all he failed to give was the name the federal anti-labor law would bear—the Taft-Hartley Act.[5]

His prediction of further attacks on freedom of thought has been confirmed many times over. The Truman administration has issued a Hitler-like decree blacklisting organizations alleged to be "subversive."[6] The demand of the Socialist Workers Party and other stigmatized organizations for a full public hearing on all charges has been disregarded by the Department of Justice.

James Kutcher, a legless war veteran, has been fired from his clerk's job in a Veterans Administration field office as a result of that blacklist.[7] An ominous thought-control purge of teachers has started at the University of Washington. Civil rights are under attack on many fronts, including the present witch-hunt trial of the Stalinists.

"All this sixty to one hundred billions of dollars that they are appropriating for the wasteful expenses of war has got to be paid for by somebody," Comrade Cannon said, "and they will try to make the masses and the poor farmers pay it." All that need be added here are the latest figures on the staggering amounts appropriated for war. The national debt stands at the fantastic sum of $260 billion, and additional billions of the national wealth are still being poured into the maw of the war machine. The rich are coining unprecedented profits from war production, while the workers and working farmers pay the piper through high taxes and robber prices.

"Demands will grow in this country, among people who want freedom and a right to live, for some way out of this madhouse of war and unemployment and growing fascism," he concluded.

The vast postwar strike wave was a preliminary confirmation of his prediction that the masses would rise in struggle against the capitalist assault on their standard of living. The defeat of the Republicans in the 1948 elections—unexpected by all the political experts and prognosticators—was due in large measure to a political uprising of the workers against the Taft-Hartley Act. Their support of Truman as the "lesser evil" by no means signified a vote of confidence in his administration. These two postwar demonstrations, one on the economic field and the other on the political, already represent down payments on Comrade Cannon's prediction of a mighty upsurge of "the people who want freedom and a right to live."[8]

These remarkable 1941 forecasts of coming events bear eloquent testimony to the validity of the true Marxist method and program that is explained by Comrade Cannon. I commend his testimony to the careful attention of the reader.

New York
February 8, 1949

NOTES

50 years of covert operations in the US

1. PAGE 31 Farrell Dobbs, *Teamster Politics* (New York: Pathfinder, 1975), p. 25 [2013 printing].

2. PAGE 46 Recounted in Charles Washburn, *A Question of Sedition* (New York: Oxford University Press, 1986), p. 90. This is one of the most substantial existing resources documenting government harassment of the Black press during World War II.

3. PAGE 47 Important part of the story of the fight against racism and political repression during World War II is told in the Pathfinder book *Fighting Racism in World War II*, a collection of articles from the *Militant*.

4. PAGE 54 Francis Biddle, *In Brief Authority* (Garden City, NY: Doubleday & Co., 1962). Biddle was not bashful about defending wiretapping. Testifying about the Bridges wiretap before the Senate Judiciary Committee in September 1941, he said, "It is a dirty business of course, but . . . we have abandoned civil rights before in time of war."

5. PAGE 61 The complete transcript of Cannon's courtroom testimony is contained in James P. Cannon, *Socialism on Trial*, published by Pathfinder.

6. PAGE 63 Patti Iiyama, "American Concentration Camps," *International Socialist Review* (April 1973), p. 28.

7. PAGE 65 More than a quarter century ago, when this article was written, it was reasonable to assume greater knowledge in the workers movement of the political record of world Stalinism than it is today.

The fact is that by the second half of the 1920s, the interests advanced and defended by the Soviet government were no longer those of the working class, either in the USSR or in countries around the world. During the early years of the Communist International, under the leadership of V.I. Lenin, those interests *had* coincided. Not because the Bolsheviks imposed their policies on other communist parties, but because all of them took as their political guide—with whatever political and organizational lapses—a common proletarian internationalist program and course.

By the period discussed in this article, however, Moscow's policies had long ago ceased to be decided by how best to advance workers' revolutionary fight for state power anywhere in the world. Instead, the Stalin regime acted to protect the material well-being and power of a social caste in the Soviet Union, one that dominated the state and party bureaucracy.

These privileged social layers had consolidated a political counterrevolution against Lenin's proletarian internationalist course. To cover up the disasters of their rightward class-collaborationist "zag" in the mid-1920s—from China, to Britain, to the Soviet countryside itself—they launched an ultraleft "zig" from 1928 through the mid-1930s.

Under the impact of the international capitalist crisis, they proclaimed, the class struggle worldwide had entered "a Third Period" of unabated "radicalization" of urban and rural workers. There could no longer be any talk of united front actions with Social Democratic organizations (now branded "social fascists"); communists had to form their own "Red" trade unions and turn their backs on the fight to transform the existing unions into instruments of revolutionary struggle; and forced collectivization of peasants in the Soviet Union was the only way to advance agricultural production and combat exploiting layers in the Soviet Union.

The calamitous outcome of that brutal, bureaucratic adventurism—first and foremost the triumph of fascism in Germany in 1933, the product above all of the Stalinists' course of blocking united resistance by the Communist and Social Democratic parties—led to yet another "zag." From 1935 on the CP leaderships pressed for "Popular Front" alliances with the bourgeois parties and governments of "democratic imperialism" the world over. A few years later—from the Stalin-Hitler Pact of August 1939 until German imperialism's invasion of the Soviet Union in June 1941—the Stalinist parties and their ranks were again ordered to make another "zig" to the left.

These abrupt shifts in Moscow's political, diplomatic, and military policies—and the expansion of its international murder machine to stamp out working-class opposition to them—not only earned Stalin the label "beheader of revolutions," but gravely endangered the defense of the Soviet Union and revolutionary conquests of workers and farmers there and around the world.

8. PAGE 67 Blas Roca's 1939 statement on adopting a "positive stance" toward Batista was published in the pamphlet *La unidad vencerá al fascismo* [Unity will conquer fascism], (Havana: Ediciones Sociales, 1939), p. 48. His approval of US ambassador Sumner Welles's assertion that the "imperialist era has ended" can be found in Roca's *Los Fundamentos del socialismo en Cuba* [Fundamentals of socialism in Cuba], (Havana: Editorial Páginas, 1943), p. 11. Roca's remarks on class collaboration cited here can be found in the pamphlet *La colaboracion entre obreros y patronos* [Collaboration between workers and employers], (Havana: Ediciones Sociales, 1945), p. 20. See also Hugh Thomas, *Cuba, or the Pursuit of Freedom* (New York: Da Capo Press, 1998), p. 734. And K.S. Karol's *Guerrillas in Power* (London: Jonathan Cape, 1971), pp. 83–87.

9. PAGE 68 An English translation of the interview with Borge was published in the *Militant*, November 14, 1986. The interview first appeared in the May 1986 issue of *Crisis*, published in Buenos Aires.

10. PAGE 77 In September 2008, twenty-one years after this article was published, Morton Sobell told *New York Times* reporter Sam Roberts that he and Julius Rosenberg had been spies for the Soviet government in the 1940s. A few days later, the Rosenbergs' two sons—Robert and Michael Meeropol—said they, too, were now convinced their father had been a spy. "I had considered that a real possibility for some time," said Robert, "and this [Sobell's statement] tips the balance."

Two years later Walter and Miriam Schneir, authors of the 1983 book *Invitation to an Inquest*, which argued that the Rosenbergs had not conducted espionage, released a second book entitled *Final Verdict: What Really Happened in the Rosenberg Case*. In it they stated their conclusion that Julius Rosenberg had begun spying for the Soviet government in 1941 and had come to head a network of eight agents.

None of this removes the stench of fabricated evidence and collusion between the judge and federal prosecutors that marked this frame up. Nor does it exculpate Washington for its unconscionable decision to execute the Rosenbergs after they rejected admitting "guilt" in return for a commutation.

The fact remains that the only charge brought against the Rosenbergs and Sobell was "conspiracy," not a single substantiated *act* of espionage. Concrete acts are much harder to demonstrate to a jury than a vague "conspiracy."

11. PAGE 77 Michael and Robert Meeropol, *We Are Your Sons* (Boston: Houghton Mifflin, 1975).

12. PAGE 94 In March 1976, the Justice Department announced new "guidelines" for FBI "counterintelligence" operations. With this cosmetic reform, the government sought to create the impression that it was curbing FBI abuses of democratic rights such as those exposed in the SWP lawsuit and other post-Watergate revelations, without restricting FBI powers in any meaningful way.

13. PAGE 105 On August 20, 1987, Judge Griesa issued an injunction prohibiting the FBI and other government agencies

from using information on the SWP and YSA that had been obtained by illegal means. He strengthened the order with a provision clarifying that the names of members of the SWP and YSA in possession of the government must have been illegally obtained, since neither organization publicly discloses such information.

In his 1986 decision, Griesa had limited his ruling on the illegality of FBI informers to the 1974–76 time period, because of the two-year statute of limitations for recovering damages.

In the injunction, however, Griesa expanded his original ruling, stating, "The court makes the finding that the informant activity for the entire period 1960–1976 was unconstitutional."

Attorney General Edwin Meese had argued that even if an injunction were to be issued, federal police agencies had to have the right to use the information contained in the sealed files in "emergency" situations, either by obtaining an exemption from any federal judge anywhere in the country, or, in cases of extreme emergency, by using the information and notifying a court later. The judge rejected this claim, stating, "no reason has been shown for allowing the Government to make an 'emergency' departure from the injunction, at its own discretion."

The injunction is a major victory for democratic rights.

Imperialist war and the working class

1. PAGE 111 Hansen's 1944 introduction is included in the sixth edition of *Socialism on Trial* issued by Pathfinder, in English and Spanish, in early 2014. Dobbs's page citations to Cannon's testimony have been changed to correspond to that new edition.

2. PAGE 111 The Communist Party leadership's support for the prosecution of the eighteen SWP and Local 544-CIO leaders is discussed earlier in this book, see pp. 17–18, 63–70. The 1948–49 Smith Act indictment and trial of the CP leaders is recounted on pp. 74–76. See also, "'An Injury to One Is an Injury to All'—A

Course Worth Defending in the Labor Movement" by Steve Clark, *New International* no. 14, pp. 223–28.

3. PAGE 112 *Socialism on Trial*, pp. 83–84.

4. PAGE 113 *Socialism on Trial*, p. 141.

5. PAGE 113 The Taft-Hartley Act, enacted in 1947, gives the federal government broad powers to intervene in and disrupt the union movement. The "Slave-Labor Act," as unionists called it, provided for court injunctions to break strikes, increased the ability of bosses and state governments to restrict union membership, outlawed work stoppages by government employees, barred secondary boycotts during labor conflicts, required union officials to sign anticommunist "loyalty" oaths, and allowed federal agencies to pry into union records and finances.

6. PAGE 113 The Attorney General's List of Subversive Organizations was issued by the Truman administration in late 1947. Before its abolition in 1974 under the pressure of the Black rights fight, anti–Vietnam War movement, and other social and political struggles in the interests of the working class, the list had grown to target almost 300 organizations. The Socialist Workers Party was included on the list from its origins.

7. PAGE 113 James Kutcher (1912–1989), who lost both legs in World War II, was fired from his federal government job in 1948. The stated reason was that he was a member of the Socialist Workers Party, which had been declared "subversive." The attack sparked an eight-year defense battle that drew support from thousands of unionists, Black rights organizations, and other supporters of political rights. In 1956 Kutcher won back his job.

8. PAGE 114 The above three quotations are from *Socialism on Trial*, p. 142.

INDEX

"60 Minutes", 12
Abt, John, 17–18
Albizu Campos, Pedro, 48
Alien and Sedition Acts, 57
American Civil Liberties Union (ACLU), 62
American Federation of Labor (AFL), 40, 53, 62
Anticommunism. See McCarthyite witch-hunt
Anti-Vietnam War movement, 9, 88
    FBI attacks on, 34, 36, 88, 90
Attorney General's List of Subversive Organizations (1947), 113, 120

Barnes, Jack, 22–23
Batista, Fulgencio, 67
Bell, Griffin, 89–90
Biddle, Francis, 45–46, 54, 58, 115
Bill of Rights, 30, 51, 53–54, 82, 91, 92, 95
Blacklisting, 25, 78, 84, 95, 113
Black Muslims, 46, 72
Black Panther Party, 43, 84
Blacks, discrimination against in US, 39–41, 46
Black struggle
    civil rights movement in US, 9, 15, 81, 84–85
    as target of FBI, 15, 34, 35, 36, 43–47, 55, 58, 88, 115
    during World War II, 39–45, 62, 64

Bolsheviks and Russian Revolution, 15, 116
Borge, Tomás, 67–68, 117
Boudin, Leonard, 25–26, 27, 83, 94–96, 98, 103–4
Bridges, Harry, 54
Britain, 34
Browder, Earl, 17, 64, 68
Brownell, Herbert, 82, 83, 90–92
Bush, George H.W., 11
Bush George W., 11

Calero, Róger, 19
Canada, in World War II, 49
Cannon, James P., 59, 60–61, 109–10, 115
Carpenter, Earl, 32
Castro, Fidel, 20–21
Chicago Defender, 45–46
Chicanos. See Mexican Americans
China, 53, 71
Civil Rights Defense Committee (CRDC), 18, 61–62, 63
Clinton, William, 11
Cointelpro (Counter-Intelligence Program), 27, 82–85, 88, 104
Cointelpro: The FBI's Secret War on Political Freedom (Nelson Blackstock), 10
Cold war, 71, 73, 74
Cologne Communist Trial (1852), 20–21
Colonial revolution, 34, 41, 51–52, 60, 71

Commager, Henry Steele, 82
Communist International, 65, 70
Communist Manifesto (Marx and Engels), 61, 99-100
Communist Party, USA
  factionalism of, 70, 74
  FBI operations against, 28, 82, 83-84, 93, 101
  lies to working class, 70, 79, 101
  and Rosenberg case (1950-53), 77-78, 101
  Smith Act trial against (1949), 17-18, 74-76, 106, 111
  and Smith Act trial of SWP (1941), 8, 17-18, 63-64, 70, 110-11
  subordination of to Soviet policies, 64-66, 69-70, 101, 116-17
  supports Roosevelt, 65-66
  "underground" during McCarthyism, 75-76, 78-79
  vulnerable to witch-hunt, 73-74, 76, 79, 101
  during World War II, 42, 62-64, 66
  See also Stalinism
Congress of Industrial Organizations (CIO), 54, 62, 65
  bureaucratization of, 53
  rise of, 33, 53
  See also Trade unions
Costa Rica, 68
Cuba, Popular Socialist Party during World War II, 66-67
Cuban Five, 21-22
Cuban Revolution, 12, 20, 21-22
Curtis, Mark, frame-up of (1988), 11, 22-23

Daily Worker, 62-64, 77, 78
Democratic Party, 51
  CP support for, 65, 66
Democratic rights
  fight to defend, 26, 30, 32, 38, 72-74, 79, 106-7
First Amendment, 25, 84-85, 96, 104
Fourth Amendment, 25-26, 91-92, 104
Democratic Socialists of America, 93
Dennis, Eugene, 76
Deportation, as weapon against working class, 11-12, 18-19, 33, 47, 54, 78
Depression, Great, 40
Dobbs, Farrell, 16-17, 31, 110-11
DuBois, W.E.B., 62
Dulles, Allen, 82

Eisenhower, Dwight, 82
Emergency Civil Liberties Committee (ECLC), 81
Engels, Frederick, 20, 61, 99
Espionage Act (1917), 12
Executive powers, expansion of, 11-12

Farmers, Black, 40
Fascism, 52
  exaggeration of threat of during McCarthyism, 75, 79
  "Popular Front" against, 60, 65, 68
FBI on Trial: The Victory in the Socialist Workers Party Suit against Government Spying (Margaret Jayko ed.), 10
Federal Bureau of Investigation (FBI)
  break-ins and wiretaps, 25, 27, 54-55, 83-84, 103, 104, 115
  cosmetic reform of, 94, 118
  files on SWP, 27, 89, 90, 97-99, 105-6
  liberal illusions in, 94, 118
  operations against SWP, 9-10, 25, 26-27, 37-38, 58, 59, 72, 82, 83-84

as political police, 14–16, 25, 32, 33–35, 36, 38, 94, 101
targets workers and farmers, 29–33, 35–36, 54
use of informers by, 26–27, 55, 84, 89, 98, 104
violates constitutional rights, 30, 54, 82, 103–4, 105, 106
See also Cointelpro
Federal Election Commission, 12–14
Fifty Years of Covert Operations in the US (Larry Seigle), 7–8, 10
Fighting Racism in World War II, 115
Final Verdict: What Really Happened in the Rosenberg Case (Walter and Miriam Schneir), 118
Foster, William Z., 75
Fouts, Howard, 32
France, 34

Garvey, Marcus, 15
Germany, 34, 39, 52, 71
González, Fernando, 21–22
González, René, 21–22
Green, Gil, 76
Griesa, Thomas, 26, 92, 95
finds attorney general in contempt (1978), 89–90
on secret government "evidence" (1981), 97–98
decision in SWP lawsuit (1986), 7, 9–10, 18, 26–27, 103–5
injunction relief by (1987), 7, 10, 27, 105–6, 118–19
Guerrero, Antonio, 21–22

Hall, Gus, 76
Hansen, Joseph, 111
Health care, 40
Hernández, Gerardo, 21–22
History Will Absolve Me (Fidel Castro), 21
Hitler, Adolf, 60–61, 66, 112
Hoover, J. Edgar, 15, 35, 54, 81–83

House Un-American Activities Committee (HUAC), 78
"I Am Prepared to Die" (Nelson Mandela), 21
Immigrants, in US, 47
See also Deportation, as weapon against working class
Immigration and Customs Enforcement (ICE), 18
Immigration and Naturalization Service (INS), 18
Internal Revenue Service (IRS), 12
Iran-contra scandal, 88

Jaffe, Philip, 17
Japan, 34, 71
Japanese Americans, 47–48, 49
Jim Crow, 40, 81, 84
Johnson, Joe, 19
Johnson, Ralph, 32

Keuch, Robert, 16, 37–38
Khrushchev, Nikita, 69
King, Martin Luther, 43
Korean War, 71, 81, 87, 88
Ku Klux Klan, 40
Kutcher, James, 113, 120

Labañino, Ramón, 21–22
Latin America
revolutionary struggle in, 34
Stalinism in, 66–68
Lenin, V.I., 61, 116
Lewis, John L., 53, 54, 62, 72

Malcolm X, 43
Maloney, Jack, 32
Mandela, Nelson, 21
Marroquín, Hector, 11, 19
Marx, Karl, 20–21, 61, 99–100
McCarran Act (1950), 75
McCarthyite witch-hunt, 34, 69, 72–74, 79–81

124 INDEX

Social Democrats and Stalinists and, 72–79
Meeropol, Michael and Robert, 118
Meese, Edwin, 27, 106, 119
Mexican Americans, 47, 88
Militant, The, 17, 46, 49, 110
Miller, Louis, 32
Muhammad, Elijah, 46

National Association for the Advancement of Colored People (NAACP), 41, 44–45, 62, 84–85, 104
National Guardian, 77
Nationalist Party (Puerto Rico), 48–49
New International, 10
Nicaragua
   Stalinists in, 67–68
   US contra war against, 88
Nixon, Richard, 9, 26, 82, 90
Northwest Organizer, 32–33

Obama, Barack, 11–12

Palmer Raids (1919–20), 19, 33
Pearl Harbor (1941), 34, 61
Pinkertons, 33
Pinto Gandía, Julio, 49
Pittsburgh Courier, 42–43, 44
Poland, 34
Political Rights Defense Fund (PRDF), 26, 27
Popular Socialist Party (PSP, Cuba), 67
Powell, Adam Clayton, 62
Privacy, right to, 26, 27, 36, 84–85, 104, 106
Puerto Ricans, 88
Puerto Rico, 48–49

Québec, conscription opposition in, 49
Quinn, Francis, 32

Randolph, A. Philip, 15
Republican Party, 51, 66
Revelations Concerning the Communist Trial in Cologne (Karl Marx), 20–21
Revolutionary Workers League (RWL, Canada), 49
Roca, Blas, 66–67
Roosevelt, Eleanor, 82
Roosevelt, Franklin D.
   attacks on labor, 15–16, 32, 33–34, 35–36, 37–38, 43–44, 54, 55, 57, 109–11
   and Japanese-American internment, 47–48
Rosenberg, Ethel and Julius, 75, 76–78, 101, 118

Schneir, Walter and Miriam, 118
Sioux City frame-up. *See* Teamsters, Midwest, and Sioux City frame-up
Skoglund, Carl, 19
Smith, Thomas, 32–33, 38
Smith Act, 30, 46, 57, 82
   trial of SWP under (1941), 15–16, 30, 46, 57–63, 109–10
   trial of CP under (1949), 17–18, 74–76, 106, 111
   purge at University of Washington under (1949), 113
Sobell, Morton, 75, 76
Social Democrats (US), 101
   See also Democratic Socialists of America; Socialist Party, USA
Socialism on Trial (James P. Cannon), 16, 21, 109–14, 119
Socialist Party, USA, 42, 72–73
Socialist Workers League (Canada), 49
Socialist Workers Party (SWP), 52, 78
   FBI operations against, 9–10, 14–

15, 25, 26–27, 36–38, 59, 72, 82, 83–84
and Federal Election Commission, 12–14
legal public activities by, 59, 96
no secret agenda of, 9, 14–15, 96, 97–100
Smith Act frame-up of (1941), 16–17, 30, 46, 57–63
Socialist Workers Party lawsuit vs. FBI, 7–10, 36–38, 82, 87, 100, 101
filing of (1973), 25–26, 87
government settlement proposed (1976–80), 93–96
attorney general found in contempt (1978), 89–90
"secret evidence" in (1981), 96–99
judge's decision in (1986), 7–10, 26–27, 103–5
monetary damages awarded (1986), 27, 104
injunction relief (1987), 7, 10, 27, 105, 105–6
federal government rules out appeal (1988), 7
and other lawsuits, 94, 95
significance of victory in, 7–8, 26, 103–5, 107
Somoza, Anastasio, 68
Soviet Union
working-class defense of, 60, 65
and world Stalinist movement, 64–70
World War II and, 39, 60, 66
See also Stalinism
Stalin, Joseph, 65–66, 69, 70
Stalin-Hitler Pact (1939), 117
Stalinism, 65–67, 116–17
"Third Period" of (1928–35), 116–17
"Popular Front" line of (1935–39), 65, 66, 67, 70, 74, 79, 117
See also Communist Party, USA;

Popular Socialist Party (PSP, Cuba)
Stulz, Walter K., 32
Sumner Welles, Benjamin, 66–67

Taft-Hartley "Slave Labor" Act (1947), 113–14
Teamster Politics (Farrell Dobbs), 31, 115
Teamsters, Midwest, Sioux City frame-up of, 29–33
Teamsters Local 544
campaign against World War II, 52–53
and Smith Act frame-up, 15–16, 30, 57, 58, 109
"Tea Party" Republicans, 12
They Have Declared Me a Man without a Country (Joe Johnson), 19
Thomas, Norman, 82
Thompson, Robert, 76
Totalitarianism, 38
Trade unions
antiwar campaigns within, 16, 51–53, 109–10, 112–13
democracy within, 58, 60
as FBI targets, 29–33, 34–36, 54, 55, 58–59, 106–7
and fight for democratic rights, 62, 79
and 1930s upsurge, 30, 33
political retreat of, 53–54, 72, 84
See also Congress of Industrial Organizations (CIO); Teamsters Local 544
Trotsky, Leon, 61, 70
Truman, Harry, administration, attacks on labor by, 113–14, 120

United Mine Workers of America (UMWA), 53, 54, 62
US government
antilabor frame-ups by, 29–33, 55–62

126   INDEX

  covert methods of, 36, 51, 83, 84, 85–88, 89, 100
  growing power of executive branch, 11–12, 15, 35, 36–37, 38, 87, 91
  and president's "inherent powers," 16, 36–37, 83, 88, 90–92, 105
  use of "subversive" charge by, 35–36, 37–38, 43–44, 51, 55, 83–84, 111, 113
  See also Federal Bureau of Investigation (FBI)
US imperialism
  response to World War I and Russian Revolution, 15, 19, 33, 36
  in World War II, 34–35, 39, 59–60
  in cold war, 71, 74
  same methods at home and abroad, 36, 87, 88
  wars inevitable under, 112
US Supreme Court, 81, 106
  on right to privacy, 85
  on wiretaps, 54–55, 91–92

Vietnam War, 88
  See also Anti-Vietnam War movement

Watergate, 9, 25, 34, 87, 88
Winston, Henry, 76
Winter, Carl, 63–64
Winter, Margaret, 97
Women, FBI and, 36, 88
Working class
  Blacks in US inside, 40–41
  FBI attacks on, 29–33, 35–36, 54
  independent political action by, 30, 65–66
  See also Trade unions
World War II, 34–35, 87, 110, 112–14
  character of, 34, 39, 60–61
  "Double V" campaign during, 43, 44, 62
  working-class opposition to, 51–53, 59–60

Youngdahl, Judge Luther, 82
Young Socialist Alliance (YSA), 7–10, 25, 26, 36, 89, 103, 104, 105

THE WORKING-CLASS STRUGGLE AND DEFENSE OF CONSTITUTIONAL FREEDOMS

Socialism on Trial
Testimony at Minneapolis Sedition Trial
JAMES P. CANNON

The revolutionary program of the working class, presented in response to frame-up charges of "seditious conspiracy" in 1941, on the eve of US entry into World War II. The defendants were leaders of the Minneapolis labor movement and the Socialist Workers Party. $15. Also in Spanish, French, and Farsi.

FBI on Trial
The Victory in the Socialist Workers Party Suit against Government Spying
MARGARET JAYKO

The record of a historic victory in the fight for political rights, including the 1986 federal court ruling against government spying and excerpts from trial testimony by SWP leaders Farrell Dobbs and Jack Barnes. $17

Cointelpro
The FBI's Secret War on Political Freedom
NELSON BLACKSTOCK

An in-depth look at the 1960s and '70s covert FBI disruption and counterintelligence program—code-named COINTELPRO. Contains reproductions of FBI documents released through the Socialist Workers Party suit against government spying. $15

PATHFINDERPRESS.COM

BUILDING A PROLETARIAN PARTY

The Low Point of Labor Resistance Is Behind Us
The Socialist Workers Party Looks Forward

JACK BARNES
MARY-ALICE WATERS
STEVE CLARK

The global order imposed by victors of the inter-imperialist slaughter of World War II is shattering, with explosive ramifications for workers and farmers worldwide. A long retreat by the working class and unions has come to an end. More and more workers of all ages, skin colors, and both sexes are saying, "Enough is enough!" This book highlights opportunities ahead for class-conscious workers to forge a labor party built on the unions. And a mass proletarian vanguard able to lead the struggle to end capitalist rule, opening a future for humanity. $10. Also in Spanish and French.

Labor, Nature, and the Evolution of Humanity
The Long View of History

FREDERICK ENGELS, KARL MARX
GEORGE NOVACK, MARY-ALICE WATERS

Without understanding that social labor, transforming nature, has driven humanity's evolution for millions of years, working people are unable to see beyond the capitalist epoch of class exploitation that warps all human relations, ideas, and values. Only the revolutionary conquest of state power by the working class can open the door to a world free of capitalist exploitation, degradation of nature, subjugation of women, racism, and war. A world built on human solidarity. A socialist world. $12. Also in Spanish and French.

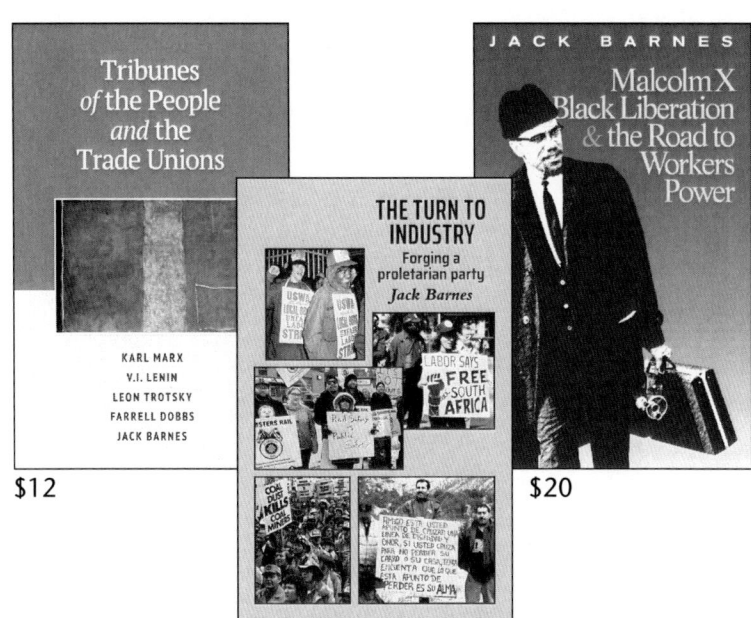

$12 $20

$15

Three books to be read as one . . .

about building a party that's working class in program, composition, and action. One that recognizes, in word and deed, the most revolutionary fact of our time . . .

. . . that working people have the power to create a different world as we act together to defend our own class interests—not those of the privileged classes who exploit our labor, not of those who fear us as "deplorables," or just plain "trash."

As we advance along a revolutionary course toward workers power, we will transform ourselves and awaken to our own worth. Also in Spanish, French, and Greek.

Special Offer!
All three $30

The Turn to Industry and *Tribunes of the People and the Trade Unions* $20

Either book plus *Malcolm X, Black Liberation, and the Road to Workers Power* $25

PATHFINDERPRESS.COM

CAPITALIST CRISIS AND THE FIGHT FOR WORKERS POWER

Are They Rich Because They're Smart?
Class, Privilege, and Learning under Capitalism
JACK BARNES

Exposes growing class inequalities in the US and the self-serving rationalizations of well-paid professionals who think their "brilliance" equips them to "regulate" working people, who don't know what's in our own best interest. $10. Also in Spanish, French, Farsi, and Arabic.

The Clintons' Anti-Working-Class Record
Why Washington Fears Working People
JACK BARNES

What working people need to know about the profit-driven course of Democrats and Republicans alike over the last three decades. And the political awakening of workers seeking to understand and resist the capitalist rulers' assaults. $10. Also in Spanish, French, Farsi, and Greek.

Is Socialist Revolution in the US Possible?
A Necessary Debate among Working People
MARY-ALICE WATERS

An unhesitating "Yes"—that's the answer given here. Possible—but not inevitable. That depends on what working people *do*. $7. Also in Spanish, French, and Farsi.

CUBA'S SOCIALIST REVOLUTION

Women in Cuba: The Making of a Revolution within the Revolution

VILMA ESPÍN
ASELA DE LOS SANTOS
YOLANDA FERRER

The integration of women in the ranks and leadership of the Cuban Revolution was intertwined with the proletarian course of the leadership of the revolution from the start. This is the story of that revolution and how it transformed the women and men who made it. $17. Also in Spanish, Farsi, and Greek.

Socialism and Man in Cuba

ERNESTO CHE GUEVARA, FIDEL CASTRO

"Man truly reaches his full human condition when he produces without being compelled by physical necessity to sell himself as a commodity," wrote Guevara in 1965. $5. Also in Spanish, French, Farsi, and Greek.

Cuba and the Coming American Revolution

JACK BARNES

This is a book about the struggles of working people in the imperialist heartland, the youth attracted to them, and the example set by the Cuban people that revolution is not only necessary—it can be made. It is about the class struggle in the US, where the revolutionary capacities of workers and farmers are today as utterly discounted by the ruling powers as were those of the Cuban toilers. And just as wrongly. $10. Also in Spanish, French, and Farsi.

PATHFINDERPRESS.COM

EXPAND YOUR REVOLUTIONARY LIBRARY

The Jewish Question
A Marxist Interpretation
ABRAM LEON

Why is Jew-hatred still raising its ugly head? What are its class roots—from antiquity through feudalism, to capitalism's rise and current crises? Why is there no solution under capitalism? The author, Abram Leon, was killed in the Nazi gas chambers. Revised translation, new introduction, and 40 pages of illustrations and maps. $17. Also in Spanish and French.

Malcolm X Talks to Young People

"The young generation of whites, Blacks, browns, whatever else—you're living at a time of revolution," said Malcolm in 1964. "And I for one will join with anyone, I don't care what color you are, as long as you want to change this miserable condition that exists on this earth." Four talks and an interview in the last months of Malcolm's life. $12. Also in Spanish, French, Farsi, and Greek.

The Communist Manifesto
KARL MARX AND FREDERICK ENGELS

Communism, say the founding leaders of the revolutionary workers movement, is not a set of ideas or preconceived "principles" but workers' line of march to power, springing from a "movement going on under our very eyes." $5. Also in Spanish, French, Farsi, and Arabic.

The Teamster Series
FARRELL DOBBS

Four books on the strikes, organizing drives, and political campaigns that transformed the Teamsters across the Midwest in the 1930s into a militant industrial union movement. Written by Farrell Dobbs, the general organizer of these Teamster battles and leader of the Socialist Workers Party.

A tool for workers seeking to use union power in every workplace and advance the fight for an independent labor party. $16 each, series $50. Also in Spanish. *Teamster Rebellion* is also available in French, Farsi, and Greek.

Cosmetics, Fashions, and the Exploitation of Women
JOSEPH HANSEN, EVELYN REED, MARY-ALICE WATERS

How big business reinforces women's second-class status and uses it to rake in profits. Where does women's oppression come from? How has the entry of millions of women into the workforce strengthened the battle for emancipation, still to be won? $12. Also in Spanish, Farsi, and Greek.

Pathfinder Press **accessible ebooks** for the blind, those with low vision, or other challenges reading print books

For a list of current accessible titles, go to: pathfinderpress.com/collections/books-for-the-blind.

Visit bookshare.org for information on how to sign up.

PATHFINDERPRESS.COM

Lenin's Final Fight
Speeches and Writings, 1922–23
V.I. LENIN

In 1922 and 1923, V.I. Lenin, central leader of the world's first socialist revolution, waged what was to be his last political battle—one that was lost following his death. At stake was whether that revolution, and the international communist movement it led, would remain on the revolutionary proletarian course that brought workers and peasants to power in October 1917. $17. Also in Spanish, Farsi, and Greek.

The Transitional Program for Socialist Revolution
LEON TROTSKY

The Socialist Workers Party program, drafted by Trotsky in 1938, still guides the SWP and communists the world over. The party "uncompromisingly gives battle to all political groupings tied to the apron strings of the bourgeoisie. Its task—the abolition of capitalism's domination. Its aim—socialism. Its method—the proletarian revolution." $17. Also in Farsi.

Thomas Sankara Speaks
The Burkina Faso Revolution, 1983–87

Under Sankara's guidance, Burkina Faso's revolutionary government led peasants, workers, women, and youth to expand literacy; to sink wells, plant trees, erect housing; to combat women's oppression; to carry out land reform; to join others worldwide to free themselves from the imperialist yoke. $20. Also in French.

Puerto Rico: Independence Is a Necessity
RAFAEL CANCEL MIRANDA

One of the five Puerto Rican Nationalists imprisoned by Washington for more than 25 years and released in 1979 speaks out on the brutal reality of US colonial domination, the example of Cuba's socialist revolution, and the ongoing struggle for independence. $5. Also in Spanish and Farsi.

New International
A MAGAZINE OF MARXIST POLITICS AND THEORY

NEW INTERNATIONAL NO. 7
Opening Guns of World War III: Washington's Assault on Iraq
JACK BARNES

The murderous assault on Iraq in 1990–91 heralded increasingly sharp conflicts among imperialist powers, growing instability of capitalism, and more wars. Also includes:

1945: When US Troops Said No!
by Mary-Alice Waters

Lessons from the Iran-Iraq War
by Samad Sharif

$14. Also in Spanish, French, and Farsi.

NEW INTERNATIONAL NO. 12
Capitalism's Long Hot Winter Has Begun
JACK BARNES

Today's global capitalist crisis is but the opening stage of decades of economic, financial, and social convulsions and class battles. Class-conscious workers confront this historic turning point for imperialism with confidence, Jack Barnes writes, drawing satisfaction from being "in their face" as we chart a revolutionary course to take power. $14. Also in Spanish, French, Farsi, Arabic, and Greek.

NEW INTERNATIONAL NO. 11
U.S. Imperialism Has Lost the Cold War
JACK BARNES

The collapse of regimes across Eastern Europe and the USSR claiming to be communist did not mean workers and farmers there had been crushed. In today's sharpening capitalist conflicts and wars, these toilers are joining working people the world over in the class struggle against exploitation. $14. Also in Spanish, French, Farsi, and Greek.

PATHFINDERPRESS.COM

PATHFINDER AROUND THE WORLD

UNITED STATES
(and Caribbean, Latin America, and East Asia)
> Pathfinder Books, 306 W. 37th St., 13th Floor
> New York, NY 10018

CANADA
> Pathfinder Books, 7107 St. Denis, Suite 204
> Montreal, QC H2S 2S5

UNITED KINGDOM
(and Europe, Africa, Middle East, and South Asia)
> Pathfinder Books, 5 Norman Rd.
> Seven Sisters, London N15 4ND

AUSTRALIA
(and New Zealand, Southeast Asia, and the Pacific)
> Pathfinder Books, Suite 2, First floor, 275 George St.
> Liverpool, Sydney, NSW 2170
> Postal address: P.O. Box 73, Campsie, NSW 2194

JOIN THE PATHFINDER READERS CLUB
BUILD YOUR LIBRARY!

$10 / YEAR
25% DISCOUNT ON ALL PATHFINDER TITLES
30% OFF BOOKS OF THE MONTH
Valid at pathfinderpress.com and local Pathfinder book centers

Go to: pathfinderpress.com/products/pathfinder-readers-club